THE GREAT AMERICAN THINKERS SERIES

This new series of original works is designed to present in highly readable form the flow of American thought from colonial times to the present. Each volume is written by a leading scholar and is devoted to a single man in the history of American thought who represents a particular trend or movement within the great span of our culture. Each book in the series contains a short biography of the man, a critical evaluation of his central ideas and their influence upon American thought as a whole, as well as an extensive bibliography and an index.

The Great American Thinkers Series is designed for the general reader as well as the serious college student or higher-level secondary school student, and is under the general editorship of two distinguished American educators: Thomas S. Knight, Ph.D., Associate Professor of Philosophy, Utica College of Syracuse University; and Arthur W. Brown, Ph.D., Chairman of the English Department and Director of the Institute of Humanities at Adelphi University. THORSTEIN VEBLEN was written by Douglas Dowd, Ph.D., Associate Professor of Economics, Cornell University.

THE GREAT AMERICAN THINKERS SERIES

The first twelve volumes in the series will be:

THOMAS JEFFERSON, by Stuart Gerry Brown, Ph.D., Maxwell Professor of American Civilization, Syracuse University.

JOHN C. CALHOUN, by Richard N. Current, Ph.D., Professor of History, University of Wisconsin.

CHAUNCEY WRIGHT, by Edward Madden, Ph.D., Professor of Philosophy, San Jose State College.

In preparation:

CHARLES PEIRCE, by Thomas S. Knight, Ph.D., Associate Professor of Philosophy, Utica College of Syracuse University.

THEODORE PARKER, by Arthur W. Brown, Ph.D., Director of the Institute of Humanities and Chairman of the English Department, Adelphi University.

WILLIAM JAMES, by Edward C. Moore, Ph.D., Graduate Dean and Coordinator of Research, University of Massachusetts.

JOHN WOOLMAN, by Edwin H. Cady, Ph.D., Rudy Professor of English, University of Indiana.

GEORGE BANCROFT, by Russel B. Nye, Ph.D., Professor of English, Michigan State University.

THORSTEIN VEBLEN, by Douglas Dowd, Ph.D., Associate Professor of Economics, Cornell University.

BENJAMIN FRANKLIN, by Ralph L. Ketcham, Ph.D., Associate Editor of the *Papers of Benjamin Franklin*, Yale University, and Professor of American Studies, Syracuse University.

JONATHAN EDWARDS, by Alfred Owen Aldridge, Ph.D., Professor of English and Director of the Program of Comparative Literature, University of Maryland.

JOHN DEWEY, by Richard J. Bernstein, Ph.D., Associate Professor of Philosophy, Yale University, and Assistant Editor of *Review of Metaphysics*.

THORSTEIN
VEBLEN

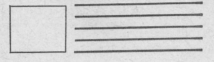

Author of this volume: Douglas Dowd, Ph.D., Associate Professor of Economics, College of Arts and Sciences, Cornell University.

Series Editors: Thomas S. Knight, Ph.D., Associate Professor of Philosophy, Utica College of Syracuse University; and Arthur W. Brown, Ph.D., Chairman of the English Department and Director of the Institute of Humanities, Adelphi University.

WASHINGTON SQUARE PRESS, INC. • NEW YORK

THORSTEIN VEBLEN

A *Washington Square Press* edition
1st printing......................September, 1964

We would like to thank the following publishers for permission to quote from several of Veblen's works:

CHARLES SCRIBNER'S SONS: Thorstein Veblen, *The Theory of Business Enterprise.*

THE VIKING PRESS, INC.: Thorstein Veblen, *The Place of Science in Modern Civilization, The Instinct of Workmanship, Imperial Germany and the Industrial Revolution, The Nature of Peace and the Terms of Its Perpetuation, The Vested Interests and the Common Man, The Engineers and the Price System, Absentee Ownership and Business Enterprise in Recent Times, Essays in Our Changing Order, The Theory of the Leisure Class, The Higher Learning in America.*

L

Published by
Washington Square Press, Inc., 630 Fifth Avenue, New York, N.Y.

WASHINGTON SQUARE PRESS editions are distributed in the U.S. by Affiliated Publishers, a division of Pocket Books, Inc., 630 Fifth Avenue, New York 20, N.Y.

FOR KAY

TABLE OF CONTENTS

Preface	xi
Chapter 1. Veblen, Man, and Society	1
Chapter 2. Veblen and American Capitalism	31
Chapter 3. Veblen and Economic Theory	55
Chapter 4. Veblen and the Main Currents of the Twentieth Century	85
Chapter 5. The Strengths and Weaknesses of Veblen	119
Appendices. On the Higher Learning Veblenisms	159
Bibliography	191
Index	197

THORSTEIN VEBLEN

PREFACE

Thorstein Veblen (1857–1929) occupies a peculiar place in the development of social science in America. If yesterday his name was prominent, today he is barely remembered; if yesterday his works were read by an influential core of intellectuals, today he is not read much, and then more by college students in literature courses than by serious students in the social sciences. Still, Veblen remains America's most noted economist, whose ideas contain much that is relevant to these turbulent times; indeed, that is why Veblen finds a place in this series of studies of Great American Thinkers.

The obscurity into which Veblen is now falling is due in part to his own shortcomings; in larger part it is due to the shortcomings of contemporary social science—not least those in economics—and to the critical attitude taken by Veblen toward the basic institutions of American society.

The present book is an attempt to rescue Veblen from undeserved neglect, and to do so by addressing the "shortcomings" just mentioned: Since Veblen's writings are profuse and somewhat less than systematic, I have attempted to distill the most important ideas from all his writings and to present them in a fashion that preserves and illuminates his meaning while compressing and reorganizing his presentation. I have attempted also to assess the validity and the limitations of Veblen's ideas by relating them to conventional economics and to contemporary economic problems. Both these points warrant elaboration.

Without doubt, Veblen was and remains the wittiest of American social scientists. Unhappily, he is remembered most for his wit; his serious side has been drowned in a wave of sly chuckles. For this turn of events, Veblen is not blameless. Perhaps, in America, the pill of serious social criticism will be swallowed only when it is coated with the sugar of humor. But if that is so, it is also true that the inner criticism must have coherence and system sufficient to make the pill effective. There *is* coherence and system in Veblen, but to appreciate it sufficiently the reader must make a sustained effort, which it is implausible to expect.

The latter is true, first, because to gain an adequate appreciation of Veblen's position no one book will suffice; each of his books requires several of the others for support and clarification of his complicated analysis. Second, the radical quality of Veblen's critique, when taken seriously, is likely to outrage the reader, whom Veblen allows to "escape" by his mode of presentation, i.e., by his wit, and by his frequent lapses into ambiguity.

Veblen's writings had consistency, but it was the consistency—if also the chaos—of a military campaign; a campaign, one must add, that the commanding general expects to lose, and which is therefore carried out with a less than maximum effort. Veblen attacked on several fronts at once: nationalism, the business system, war, *de facto* political oligarchy, a corrupted educational system, and, most generally, irrationality. All these Veblen included under a recurring expression: "force and fraud." Veblen's half-hearted attempt to provide a coherent picture of his strategy leaves the reader of any *one* of his books in a position much like that of a lieutenant in a battle—possessed of only part of the "big picture." This difficulty in Veblen was integrally related to his analytical approach; it stemmed from a respectful recognition of social complexity, and from some combination of skepticism and despair. As Veblen so often said of others, he had the defects of his virtues.

Second, social scientists in general, and economists in particular, tend to work *within* the social institutions of their time and place, rather than, as Veblen thought was their function, to regard such institutions as a scientist does his data, i.e., from the outside. It is true, of course, that social scientists are a *part* of the data they study (whereas a physicist, say, is not, in any relevant sense) and they cannot wholly detach themselves from their objects of study. Veblen was a part of the society he analyzed also; but Veblen did not take basic institutions as *given*, as do many contemporary social scientists.

Veblen took institutions—their origins, their nature, their functioning, their interrelationships—as the prime focus of the social scientist; as the matters most to be *questioned*. To do this necessarily makes the social scientist a social critic, to one degree or another. This in turn implies that the social scientist, to one degree or another, willy-nilly becomes embroiled in controversy. Professional economists have not taken up the challenges thrown down by Veblen chiefly because to do so would involve them in social controversy to a degree that most find unseemly, as well as unnecessary. More often than not, Veblen said of social scientists in *The Higher Learning in America,* "their intellectual horizon is bounded by the same limits of commonplace insight and preconceptions as are the prevailing opinions of the conservative middle class" (p. 136).

What has just been said is likely to strike the professional as wrong-headed, while the layman may be surprised that such questions need even arise. The professional is inclined and habituated to view his work in a manner that places Veblen's approach outside, or at the fringes, of the discipline. The layman, disturbed by the immense and urgent problems of the day, is likely to find Veblen insightful and provocative and to be prompted to take the next steps of fruitful inquiry. If the layman is a college student, he will only rarely find the "next steps" being taken in his college courses in social science. This book has been written partially in the hope that serious students will do something to change this situation, if only by raising "Veblenian" questions with their instructors and in their own professional work.

If it is true that several of Veblen's books must be read for the strength of his position to be appreciated, it is also true that more than the present book must be read. In attempting to introduce more order into Veblen's writings than he himself provided, I have allowed myself to presume that I may usefully provide a procedural guide for those who are stimulated to read further. There are eleven books* containing Veblen's writings. (In the bibliography these books are prefaced by Roman numerals, the purpose of which is to identify the source of quotations in the text.) Of Veblen's eleven books, four are collections of articles and essays. One of these, *The Place of Science in Modern Civilization*, can be read most meaningfully only if the reader has some training in economics. The essays are almost entirely critical of conventional thought; given an understanding of what that thought is, the essays contain some of Veblen's most rigorous and helpful contributions.

Apart from the latter, I believe that the following order is best designed to provide the new reader of Veblen with a coherent presentation of his major ideas:

1. *The Theory of the Leisure Class*
2. *The Instinct of Workmanship*
3. *The Theory of Business Enterprise*
4. *Absentee Ownership and Business Enterprise in Recent Times*
5. *Imperial Germany and the Industrial Revolution*
6. *An Inquiry into the Nature of Peace and the Terms of Its Perpetuation*

Not everyone would agree with this order, of course; some have suggested that the essays collected in *The Vested Interests and the Common Man* be read first, for example. It is my view that the latter essays, and those in *The Engineers and the Price System* and in *Essays in Our Changing Order* are best read after grasping Veblen's fundamental ideas.

One of Veblen's books has yet to be listed: *The Higher Learning in America*. This is one of Veblen's most carefully written books; at least one of Veblen's interpreters thinks it is his most valuable contribution. It is a book that stands somewhat off to the side of Veblen's other works, if Veblen is taken to be an economist. Be that as it may, *The Higher*

---

*Excluding *The Laxdæla Saga*, Veblen's translation of an Icelandic work that is not of interest in this connection.

Learning may be read independently without suffering significant loss of Veblen's meaning, although an appreciation of Veblen's view of business enterprise is closely relevant, given his concern with the influence on the university of businessmen and business values.

Few can read Veblen's searching critiques of American society without wondering what, if anything, he had in mind as an alternative. Later, I shall point out that Veblen frequently refers to "industrial democracy" as a desirable form of social organization, with emphasis both on the adjective and the noun. But Veblen did little in the way of going beyond this term as indication of a "program," and it is a term that many and diverse reformers have found suitable. One learns from Veblen what particular institutions he thought "imbecilic"; much of this book is concerned to show just that. However, one cannot deduce some symmetrically "opposite" set of social institutions that might show what *particular institutions* Veblen would support. He was "for" peace, the use of modern technology, science, democracy, and the like; but these are not "particular institutions."

Veblen did make it clear that he thought a position of strategic importance should be held by technically competent personnel (e.g., engineers) in a sane society; he also made it quite clear that capitalist institutions are generally unsuited and even dangerous, if economic and social welfare are to be maintained over time. Similarly, his pronouncements against the nation-state are clear and unequivocal. But to be against, say, capitalism, is not *necessarily* to be for, say, socialism. What then was Veblen "for"?

Many have attempted to answer that question. An accurate answer requires a prior understanding that Veblen spent virtually none of his time talking or writing in programmatic terms, if only because of his view of how the process of social change takes place (for which, see Chapter 1). Readers impressed by Veblen's vigorous criticisms must expect to gain little of an idea from Veblen of what might desirably take the place of the institutions he deplored. Only the most general of statements can be made on this question, and I shall give my own interpretation, for what it is worth.

Veblen seems to have held *loosely* to a goal most closely approximated by the program of Guild Socialism advocated in Great Britain before World War I. This would have held the power of the state to a minimum, and provided for worker control of a decentralized industrial economy. I say "loosely" because the foregoing contradicts one of Veblen's dearly held ideas; namely, that the modern industrial technology requires a high degree of centralized coordination. Whether or not this is a real conflict, Veblen did not reconcile it in his writings. He did sketch out his views on international organization in the absence of strong nation-states in *The Nature of Peace*, and they are still worth reading.

The fact that Veblen had no "blueprint" for social reform has allowed his followers to interpret him as being everything from a conservative to a radical, from a nihilist to a revolutionary socialist. Not only did Veblen lack a program, he had little faith in political activism, and he practiced it even less. His contribution to the present generation is not in what he proposed, for he proposed virtually nothing. It is rather his analysis of what is "wrong" and why that has meaning for today.

The attempt to interpret the works of any great thinker runs unavoidable risks, and unavoidably the finished product strikes some as extreme, others as flaccid. If risks cannot be avoided, they can be somewhat reduced by gaining the help of competent and sympathetic colleagues. I have been much helped by, and should like to express my heartfelt gratitude to, two of my colleagues. Malcolm Liggett, now at the University of California at Santa Barbara, read through the entire manuscript assiduously and with intelligent and informed appreciation, as one of those very rare young economists who is thoroughly familiar with Veblen's approach. His understanding and his desire to see Veblen's ideas presented as clearly as possible have done much to eliminate confusions that might otherwise have been propagated by me. Alfred E. Kahn of Cornell University read two chapters critically, but not without sympathy; his comments were most useful in eliminating certain imbalances of interpretation and in furnishing perspective on important current issues. I should also like to thank the editors of this series, Professors Arthur W. Brown and Thomas S. Knight, for their careful and most helpful suggestions and corrections concerning both form and substance.

Confusions doubtless remain; some due to inadequacies on my part, some due to my stubbornness on particular issues. In this latter respect I share an attitude of Professor Melvin M. Knight, a former mentor: "Who would knowingly read the book of any person entirely lacking in opinions from which all attempts to dislodge him are vain?"

D.F.D.

Ithaca, N.Y.
June, 1964

Chapter 1

VEBLEN, MAN, AND SOCIETY

Thorstein Bunde Veblen, more than a generation after his death in 1929, remains what he was in life: America's most controversial social scientist. Veblen is less discussed and less influential now than in the twenties and thirties; but when and where his ideas are still debated, controversy runs deep. Veblen threw down the gauntlet of radical social criticism to the complacent. He was both the chronicler and the analyst of what today we call "the sick society." His conclusions challenged the basic institutions of modern society; his analysis challenged the basic procedures of social science.

Veblen was a radical in the fullest sense of the term: he took nothing as sacred, nothing as given. He was not, however, a political radical nor a reformer—although more than one radical or reform group looked upon him as the source of its leading principles. For reasons going deep into his temperament and his theoretical outlook, Veblen was basically indifferent, even scornful, of attempts to translate his ideas into political programs. He seemed content to probe and to report, as though his aim were merely to dislodge irritating matter from his system. What his readers might do with his ideas, if anything, was their affair. As for Veblen, he was almost entirely resigned to the notion that the world was persistently and ineluctably bent on folly and associated major or minor disasters.

Thorstein Veblen was a child during the Civil War, and an old man during World War I. He was born on a farm in Wisconsin, the son of Norwegian immigrants. In the 1870's, when he left the farm and began his development as an intellectual, America was in the early years of a period of severe agrarian discontent that was not to end until the turn of the century. The farmers' turmoil was a product of rapid and spectacular economic, political, and social developments within and outside America. The farmers were caught off guard and angered by what they took to be threats to their material welfare, social status and political power. They struck out at those they took to be their enemies: the industrial monopolist, the financier, the speculator, the kept politician.

Veblen's targets were similar to those of the farmer, but his list was longer, and more general, and included the farmer himself. More importantly, Veblen's *analysis* parted company with his rural background in its aims, its nature, its depth, and its implications. Veblen was a scholarly radical; he was not an agrarian reformer.

Doubtless Veblen's roots in a farm family provided initial impetus to his later investigations. But his keen intellect, his remarkable range of knowledge, and an ingrained dour viewpoint made Veblen one of the great minds of his generation, rather than merely an angry and literate farmer. Veblen was immersed in the latest currents of thought in philosophy, history, economics, sociology, psychology, anthropology, engineering, and more. His genius consisted of putting the various aspects of his knowledge into a comprehensive analytical framework, the aim of which was to delineate the process of social change.

Consider the manner in which America changed in Veblen's lifetime. In 1857, the year he was born, America was a predominantly commercial-agrarian society, just emerging into its industrializing phase, characterized still by the relatively small-scale merchant and farmer. By 1929, the year Veblen died, America was the world's leading industrial power, giddy in what it took to be permanent prosperity— until the last month or two of that year. America had become urbanized, if not urbane; its economy, and much else, was dominated by large-scale organization and control in industry, finance, and trade. And, symbolically, while in the 1920's industry and finance gave every appearance of flourishing, the lot of the independent farmer was one of great and increasing difficulties—as measured by persistent overproduction and sagging markets, growing tenancy, spreading bankruptcy, and attempts to gain remedial farm legislation, all in the "prosperity decade."

While America changed, so too did the rest of the world. The decades after our Civil War saw the rapid spread of industrialization from England to continental Europe, Japan, and of course to North America. Concomitantly, a wave of imperialism conquered virtually the entire globe, nationalism spread feverishly, and a rapid growth of technology allowed and required cheap and large-scale production of fuels, metals, and machinery. Through the spread and improvement of transportation and communications facilities, in this period the entire world was tied into one interdependent economy.

These worldwide developments—combining industrialism, capitalism, nationalism, and imperialism—were neither all to the good nor all to the bad. Their promise was a function of the same factors as the dangers contained within them. More fully than any American before or since, Veblen grasped the nature of both the threats *and* the promises; it became his life's work to show which was which, and why.

To this end, Veblen attempted to explain the principal determinants of individual and social behavior (in *The Theory of the Leisure Class,* and in *The Instinct of Workmanship*); the principal determinants of a capitalist economy (in *The Theory of Business Enterprise*); and the principal determinants of international violence (in *The Nature of Peace*). These four books constitute the foundation of Veblen's thought. His many other books and essays are largely applications or extensions of the ideas contained in the books cited—with the possible exception of his technical essays in economic theory.

Veblen adopted the role of the dispassionate spectator in his writings: the scientist who merely observes, describes, and analyzes. He took pains to disclaim any judgment—favorable or unfavorable—on the matters he discussed, and the disclaimer was the more likely to be forthcoming as the vigor of his criticism mounted. Neutrality—as distinct from honesty and procedural scruples—is probably not to be expected in the examination of social processes. Because the objects of Veblen's ironic approbation or opprobrium are quite consistent throughout his writings, one cannot take his self-styled neutrality seriously. But there is a quality in Veblen's thought that sets him apart from most other social scientists. It is the quality of the outsider. Although Veblen doubtless had strong preferences in the matter of social organization, he stood seemingly aloof from the matters he analyzed. In Veblen this may be interpreted as the detachment of despair.

In Veblen's analysis social change is a continuous evolutionary process; although changes are initiated and guided by men, they emerge from a pattern of deep-seated habituation; even the most deliberately wrought "revolutionary" changes so mix reason with unreason as to leave man unwittingly and largely captive to his past—a past whose hand is heavy, the more so as its weight goes unnoticed. Seeing things so, Veblen placed himself apart from the developments he analyzed and assumed the role of Cassandra.

Veblen was an outsider throughout his life. He was born an outsider in the rural midwest, the son of an immigrant Norwegian farmer. As he grew older, he remained an outsider by choice, deliberately rejecting conventional personal and professional relationships. He set himself against the mainstream of life in his day.

To say that Veblen was the son of a farmer is not, however, to suggest a typically bucolic family environment. Thomas Veblen, Thorstein's father, was abreast of the most modern agricultural methods of his time, and he had a regard for the life of the mind that distinguished him not only from other farmers but also from the urban folk of his day. Young Thorstein was sent to Carleton College, one of the fine small colleges of America, at a time when very few young people were fortunate enough to attend college.

Veblen subsequently went on to graduate school—at Johns Hopkins, Yale, and Cornell, studying philosophy and economics—and earned a Ph.D. degree. The picture of a rude western farm boy attending some of the best eastern universities of his day, in a period of bustling industrialization, helps to explain the outsider characteristics of Veblen's personality.

Veblen's undergraduate and graduate studies were concentrated in the field of philosophy. At that time philosophy embraced more than it does today—reaching out to include religion at one end and social studies at the other. The great economists of the nineteenth century—Malthus, Ricardo, John Stuart Mill, Marx, Marshall—were not the narrow specialists we know as economists today. Doubtless the breadth of view thus suggested was not all to the good; be that as it may, in Veblen's day the trend toward narrow specialization in economics was well under way, and much of Veblen's writings in and around the field of economics may be construed as running against that trend.

Indeed, one of the enduring controversies centering around Veblen's ideas concerns just this issue: what are the appropriate scope and method of economics? Or, can one arrive at meaningful conclusions in economics without lengthening its grasp to include the past, and broadening its focus to contain "non-economic" (e.g., legal, sociological, psychological, political) behavior?

Veblen's first publication (1884) belonged in one of the narrower corridors of philosophy, but his next (1891) and almost all that followed were directly or indirectly concerned with the theoretical and practical economic issues of his day. Despite the fact that the subject matter of much of Veblen's writings—culture, war, sports, religion—is seemingly outside the scope of economics, Veblen took economic affairs as central in determining human behavior.

The economic life history of any community is its life history in so far as it is shaped by men's interest in the material means of life. This economic interest has counted for much in shaping the cultural growth of all communities. . . . The economic interest goes with men through life. . . . It affects the cultural structure at all points, so that all institutions may be said to be in some measure economic institutions (VIII, 76-77).*

The first and most basic of all Veblen's books is *The Theory of the Leisure Class* (1899). Although it provides the best introduction to Veblen's thought, it is more than an introduction. In it almost all his major ideas, and hints of most of the ideas he developed in later writings can be found. *The Theory of the Leisure Class* may be viewed as an extended essay in social psychology and anthropology, whose aim, however, is to provide a reasonable basis for economic analysis.

Today, Veblen's psychological and anthropological theories often seem quaint, or worse; but much of what he had to say about man's inclinations, and resulting social processes, has an enduring quality and much of it has been borne out by subsequent, "more scientific" studies. What Veblen lacked in today's techniques and methods, he made up in insight. Like other great thinkers, Veblen's creative imagination sometimes led him into error; but, like other great social philosophers, he is also remembered for his many insightful generalizations. Had he followed his own rules and confined himself to plausible empirical investigations, the limitations of his time and the techniques of his day, ironically, would have reduced his intellectual contributions to a mundane level.

The basic concepts in *The Theory of the Leisure Class* are three: the leisure class, conspicuous consumption (and conspicuous waste), and pecuniary emulation. It is these institutions or behavior patterns, and the process in which

---

* Here it is appropriate to have Veblen specify what he means by the important term "institutions": They are, "in substance, prevalent habits of thought with respect to particular relations and particular functions of the individual and of the community; and the scheme of life, which is made up of the aggregate of institutions in force at a given time or at a given point in the development of any society, may, on the psychological side, be broadly characterized as a prevalent spiritual attitude or a prevalent theory of life . . ., in the last analysis reducible to terms of a prevalent type of character" (I, 190).

they merge and interact, that Veblen found indispensable to an understanding of social development.* These in turn rest on an even more fundamental notion: man's need for self-respect. The power of the leisure class, the pervasiveness of conspicuous consumption, and the strength of pecuniary emulation are rooted in this need for self-respect. For Veblen,

> the usual basis of self-respect is the respect accorded by one's neighbors. Only individuals with an aberrant temperament can in the long run retain their self-esteem in the face of the disesteem of their fellows. Apparent exceptions to the rule are met with, especially among people with strong religious convictions. But these apparent exceptions are scarcely real exceptions, since such persons commonly fall back on the putative approbation of some supernatural witness of their deeds (I, 30).

Veblen's ideas concerning the leisure class, conspicuous consumption and emulation, self-respect (and status), published in 1899, continue to have great explanatory use in the conforming and "affluent" society of the mid-twentieth century.

What is the leisure class, and who is in it? How did it arise? What rôle does it play? The prime requisite for membership in the leisure class (i.e., propertied, non-industrial), ancient or modern, is "exemption from industrial employments"—where the term "industrial," as used by Veblen, means involvement in actual physical production, as distinct, say, from salesmanship. Where the line would be drawn in today's complicated, highly specialized, and increasingly white-collar economy might be impossible to specify exactly; Veblen would probably have been content to draw it where the manipulation of people and property (the function of the leisure class) is distinguished from the manipulation of

---

* As Veblen used words, "emulation" is the *motive* that leads to the *acts* of conspicuous behavior. In practice the motive and the action may be indistinguishable.

"things" (the function of industry). As Veblen defined it, leisure class society "depends on the growth of technical knowledge and the use of tools"—in current terms, it depends on the development of social productivity to the point where a surplus over current consumption needs is feasible. Modern anthropologists—and Veblen would concur—would place such a development somewhere in the Stone Age, in barbarian society.* Under such circumstances, a non-productive class, specialized in some such function as shaman or warrior, could consume without producing.

Veblen does not suggest that because the leisure class is "unproductive" it plays an *unimportant* rôle in society—far from it—but merely that the rôle played is dependent upon exploit, prowess, fraud, or force, rather than direct participation in the productive process. Thus, in the societies Veblen classified as barbarian, the leisure class is made up of hunters and warriors, and

the women do what other work there is to do—other members who are unfit for man's work [i.e., hunting and fighting] being for this purpose classed with the women. But the men's hunting and fighting are both of the same general character. Both are of a predatory nature; the warrior and hunter alike reap where they have not strewn. Their aggressive assertion of force and sagacity differs obviously from the women's assiduous and uneventful shaping of materials [e.g., farming, cloth-making, pottery]; it is not to be accounted productive labor, but rather an acquisition of substance by seizure . . . [and] any effort that does not involve an assertion of prowess comes to be unworthy of man (I, 14).

* Veblen, in keeping with cultural anthropologists before and since his time, classified societies into savage, barbarian, and civilized, a distinction based primarily on technological and economic characteristics. A savage society is one dependent on hunting and gathering, a barbarian society has developed a settled agriculture with domesticated plants and animals and village life (among other things), and a civilized society is one characterized by a more complicated technology combined with relatively great specialization, writing, urbanization, and so on.

The leisure class is not an indolent class; it is a class of property owners or, more generally, a class with claims on the production of others. For Veblen, the first ownership and associated set of claims was that of ownership or enslavement of woman by man. The historical accuracy of such a view probably cannot be verified, but it is entirely plausible that slavery (whether of women or men and women) constituted an early, if not the first, form of wealth, that it was a product of force, and that its existence made possible an unproductive class—as, e.g., in Ancient Egypt, where the leisure class was the priesthood.*

It would perhaps not do to take Veblen's ideas literally. Still, even in contemporary society, that man is more honorable and his status higher who is farthest removed from working with his hands—be he tycoon, minister, general, statesman, or, as Veblen put it, "public Merrymaker." Veblen's concepts of conspicuous consumption and pecuniary emulation are clearly applicable in our own day, particularly to Americans. We seek to convince others—and ourselves—of our worth by a demonstrably wasteful standard of living, and do what we can to become "exempt from industrial pursuits." To be sure, much of this is true because some wasteful consumption is pleasurable, and most industrial pursuits are poorly paid, monotonous, and even dangerous. But when our pleasure is derived from the attitudes of others (real or presumed) toward our consumption, and when we avoid working with our hands even when such activities are not poorly paid, monotonous, or dangerous, it is emulation, or "honorific calculation," that motivates us. What proportions of our consuming and producing activities are "invidiously motivated," it would be impossible to say; it would not be immoderate, however, to state that neither the quantitative nor the qualitative aspects of our economic (and much of our non-economic) life are intelli-

---

* That the priesthood in Ancient Egypt owed its position "originally" to an understanding of the flooding pattern of the Nile is often asserted. Whether or not that is so, the persistence of the priests' ability to consume without producing anything but ceremony, ritual, and devout observances, in Veblen's eyes would constitute a form of fraud, probably mixed with force.

gible if consumption and production are viewed primarily as means of satisfying physical needs.

Veblen found the origins of the leisure class in the functions of warrior and hunter (or priest). But soon, in the evolution of barbarism, and with the development of production, the ownership of property—initially booty, or trophies of conquest—comes to be taken as the prime mark of honor and prowess.

Not that esteem ceases to be awarded on the basis of other, more direct evidence of prowess; not that successful predatory aggression or warlike exploit ceases to call out the envy of the less successful competitors; but the opportunities for gaining distinction by means of this direct manifestation of superior force grow less available both in scope and frequency. At the same time opportunities for industrial aggression, and for the accumulation of property by the quasi-peaceable methods of nomadic industry, increase in scope and availability. And it is even more to the point that property now becomes the most easily recognized evidence of a reputable degree of success as distinguished from heroic or signal achievement. It therefore becomes the conventional basis of esteem. Its possession in some amount becomes necessary in order to any reputable standing in the community (I, 28-29).

At the apex of the leisure class is the ruling class. It is the class that runs the show, that consumes without producing, that sets society's standards; and that accomplishes all this and more by some combination of "force and fraud." Veblen was deeply affected by a sense of ubiquitous social injustice—although he would never have put it so. Like others, Veblen posited an early state of social development where man lived in a (savage) state of peace and quiet—in effect, in a stage of primitive communism. He found, or thought he found, such societies in his own time, among the Andaman Islanders, the Todas, the Ainu, and others. In such groups, Veblen asserted, the following characteristics are prevalent:

> [They are] . . . without a leisure class. . . . They are small groups and of a simple archaic structure; they are commonly peaceable and sedentary; they are poor; and individual ownership is not a dominant feature of their economic system. . . . The most notable trait common to members of such communities is a certain amiable inefficiency when confronted with force or fraud (I, 7).*

Whatever the merits or demerits of such a view of the past, Veblen had no desire or expectation that modern society would ever return to that pristine state. He did have hopes, however slender, that the invidious, violent, and irrational aspects of modern life could be diminished, largely through the growth of a "matter-of-fact" point of view among the "underlying population," made possible by the growth of science and technology, day-to-day life in an industrial society, and the instinct of workmanship (to be examined later). But the prime obstacle to such a progression is the modern leisure class.

The modern leisure class most interested Veblen. For him, it was principally the business class—the class that controls the wealth and sets the tone of modern industrial society. Military, religious, and political functionaries are also members of the modern leisure class, but they are secondary in power and derivative in function to the class of business leaders. Veblen saw the modern business leader as essentially a latter-day predatory warrior—transformed,

---

* Veblen was under no illusions as to the survival power of such "amiable" societies, in a world in which they are exceptional. In speaking, for example, of medieval Iceland, a society apparently largely devoid of aggressive characteristics, Veblen says, ". . . it died of legal friction and constitutional formalities after some experience at the hands of able and ambitious statesmen in contact with an alien government drawn on the coercive plan. The clay vessel failed to make good among the iron pots, and so proved its unfitness to survive in the world of Christian nations . . ." (V, 13).

armed, and clothed in a fashion that enables him to dominate modern industrial society.

> The relation of the leisure . . . class to the economic process is a pecuniary relation—a relation of acquisition, not of production; of exploitation, not of serviceability. Indirectly their economic office may, of course, be of the utmost importance to the economic life process; and it is by no means intended to depreciate the economic function of the propertied class or of the captains of industry. The purpose is simply to point out what is the nature of the relation of these classes to the industrial process and to economic institutions. Their office is of a parasitic character, and their interest is to divert what substance they may to their own use, and to retain whatever is under their hand. The conventions of the business world have grown up under the selective surveillance of this principle of predation or parasitism. They are conventions of ownership; derivatives, more or less remote, of the ancient predatory culture (I, 209).

The relationship between the leisure class and the non-leisure class is the prime determinant of the quality of society and of the rate and direction of social change, as Veblen saw it; and his analysis of this question gives his writings their most distinctive quality. Two other factors of first-rank importance appear repeatedly in Veblen's social analysis: technological change and the instinct of workmanship. These act as constructive elements in the process of social change; but they are constantly perverted by irrational factors rooted in the dominance of the leisure class and the emulative behavior of the common man. Veblen's hopes for the future were based on the remote possibility that the rational in man would triumph over the irrational as a result of the spread and use of modern technology, guided by the instinct of workmanship.

But Veblen had few such optimistic moments. Beginning with his gloomy essay on socialism, written in 1891, and ending with his harsh and bitter final book *Absentee Ownership*, written in 1923, Veblen saw rational inclinations subdued, diverted, and "contaminated" by man's atavistic predatory inclinations and by the nature and powers of the leisure class.

In *The Theory of the Leisure Class*, conspicuous consumption and pecuniary emulation are given their rôle and meaning insofar as they relate to the leisure class. Here we return to the importance of self-respect in Veblen's view. Veblen's treatment of self-respect was not, nor was it intended to be, comprehensive. He was concerned only to show the part it played in the determination of basic social patterns. As indicated earlier, for all but the "aberrant," self-respect is something gained in society through the esteem in which one is held by others.*

Since it is the leisure class that is above all the class held in repute by the community, the principal means of gaining self-respect is to be viewed as belonging to that class. This purpose—whether conscious or unconscious is irrelevant —is the principal determinant of both the consuming and producing activities of leisure-class society. As such, it is the set of relationships against which the functioning of the economy—and much else besides—must be understood. The motivation underlying consumption expenditures is indirect. We do not consume in order to satisfy our basic needs for comfort and survival—although that is of course a part of everyone's consuming activities—but in order to create a decorous appearance. And the appearance sought for is the appearance of membership in the leisure class.** In one

---

* See, for example, the remark of J. Robert Oppenheimer, when he was awarded the Atomic Energy Commission's Enrico Fermi Prize: "Most of us look to the good opinion of our colleagues and to the good will and the confidence of our Government. I am no exception," *New York Times*, April 4, 1963.

** Veblen was of course aware that what is meant by "comfort" or even "survival" is defined variously in different societies, and variously in any one society at different stages in its development. This variation strengthens rather than weakens his point, for it points to the cultural or socio-psychological bases of such definitions. Veblen also argued that the percentage of consumption devoted to such "real needs" declines in favor of expenditures whose purpose is to satisfy social aspiration, as the economy advances.

of his many witty and suggestive phrases, Veblen underlined this notion by pointing out that "it is by no means an uncommon occurrence, in an inclement climate, for people to go ill clad in order to appear well dressed" (I, 168).

The leisure class is the class of wealth: the class that consumes without direct production, by virtue of ownership, status, "force or fraud." To seem a member of this class, one must create the appearance of affluence in his dress, demeanor and living arrangements, and, as well, provide an impression of "exemption from all useful employment." These purposes are fulfilled by activities Veblen classified as "conspicuous leisure," "conspicuous waste," and, among others and most generally, "conspicuous consumption."

In an important passage, Veblen argued that, "In order to gain and to hold the esteem of men it is not sufficient merely to possess wealth or power. The wealth or power must be put in evidence, for esteem is awarded only on evidence" (I, 36).

It is not fact, but appearance that counts. Appearance is evident, and the evidence may take many and different forms: dress, housing, "conspicuous abstention from labor," "decorous behavior" and other signs of "good breeding," such as quasi-scholarship, participation in civic projects of obviously limited utility, and so on. The evidence may also be indirect. "Vicarious leisure," e.g., the hobbling dress or social activities of one's wife (for Veblen, woman had not fully emerged from her early status as property) by indicating helplessness or the ability to waste, lends status to the husband. Such also is the derivative leisure or waste of the servant class. And "since vicarious leisure is possible only on the basis of status or of hired service, the disappearance of the relation of status from human intercourse at any point carries with it the disappearance of vicarious leisure . . ." (I, 66).

For a further listing of the types of behavior Veblen cited to illustrate the many facets of leisure class emulation, the reader may delight himself by consulting Veblen directly. But one additional point of importance remains. Veblen does not find a simple two-class society: leisure class and non-leisure class. Although he uses that terminology, he is as much concerned with the many strata within each large grouping. Thus, within the leisure class proper there are, for example, the settled aristocracy and the *nouveau riche*. The latter emulate (and gradually replace) the former, and the former despise the pretensions—and the usually greater wealth—of the latter.

Within the substantial bulk of the population that belongs to the non-leisure class, there is of course even more considerable stratification. Veblen saw the members of each sub-group straining to lose their identity with their own group, and seeking to be identified with the group immediately "above" their own—i.e., next closest to the leisure class proper. The picture thus drawn is one of pervasive discontent and striving, where the *standard* of living is the level of living of those above one's own social class. This standard acts much as the carrot placed in front of the donkey's nose. It provides the motive for unremitting effort to change one's life, however comfortable or adequate the current *level* of life might be, in the absence of pecuniary emulation.

In Veblen's words,

the standard of expenditure which commonly guides our efforts is not the average, ordinary expenditure already achieved; it is an ideal of consumption that lies just beyond our reach, or to reach which requires some strain. The motive is emulation—the stimulus of an invidious comparison which prompts us to outdo those with whom we are in the habit of classing ourselves (I, 103).

Pecuniary emulation, combined with economic possibilities, makes for a further important characteristic of consumer expenditures:

The standard is flexible; and especially it is indefinitely extensible, if only time is allowed for habituation to any increase in pecuniary ability and for acquiring facility in the new and larger scale of expenditure that follows such an increase. It is much more difficult to recede from a scale of expenditure once adopted than it is to extend the accustomed scale in response to an accession of wealth (I, 102).

The strength with which Veblen held these views is revealed by the following observation:

With the exception of the instinct of self-preservation, the propensity for emulation is probably the strongest and most alert and persistent of the economic motives proper. In an industrial community this propensity for emulation expresses itself in pecuniary emulation; and this, so far as regards the Western civilized communities of the present, is virtually equivalent to saying that it expresses itself in some form of conspicuous waste (I, 110).

Finally, lest his predominantly academic readers feel themselves exempt from these irrationalities, Veblen, speaking of the "classes given to scholarly pursuits," says,

because of a presumed superiority and scarcity of the gifts and attainments that characterize their life, these classes are by convention subsumed under a higher social grade than their pecuniary grade should warrant. The scale of decent expenditure in their case is pitched correspondingly high, and it consequently leaves an exceptionally narrow margin disposable for the other ends of life . . . ; there is no class of the community that spends a larger proportion of its substance in conspicuous waste than these (I, 113-14).

If the role and meaning of the leisure class, and of its emulation by others, were confined to conspicuous consumption in its various manifestations, Veblen's analysis could be dismissed as merely one more sour view of human foibles.

But Veblen does not propose to stop there. There is more to be said of the leisure class and larger inferences remain to be drawn. For the sake of brevity these latter will be discussed as they bear on the process of social change, through the situation, actions, and attitudes of (1) the working class and (2) the leisure class.

Veblen did not view the working class (= industrial class = common man = underlying population) as entirely captive to conspicuous consumption and all that it connotes; nor did he attribute all conspicuous consumption to emulation of the leisure class. He did see the industrial class, by virtue of its productive function and by virtue of its constant exposure to the exigencies and hardships of modern industrial society, as being in the most likely position to feel the need for and demand an alteration in social institutions. Out of such an environment Veblen saw trade unionist and socialist movements arising. But, if the working class was so motivated, its aims, Veblen believed, were muddied by the substantial infusion of pecuniary motives in its own producing activities, by its aping of leisure-class standards and by its attraction to patriotism and religion. In any event, its power to bring about change was limited by the crippling weaknesses of simply being poor.

The abjectly poor, and all those persons whose energies are entirely absorbed by the struggle for daily sustenance, are conservative because they cannot afford the effort of taking thought for the day after tomorrow; just as the highly prosperous are conservative because they have small occasion to be discontented with the situation as it stands today (I, 204).

For those who are not "abjectly poor," claimed Veblen, the reputability of the leisure class—in addition to all else, the politically most conservative class—sets the political standard:

The fact that the usages, actions, and views of the well-to-do leisure class acquire the character of a prescriptive canon of conduct for the rest of society, gives added weight and reach to the conservative influence of that class. It makes it incumbent upon all reputable people to follow their lead. So that, by virtue of its high position as the avatar of good form, the wealthier class comes to exert a retarding influence upon social development far in excess of that which the simple numerical strength of the class would assign it. Its prescriptive example acts to greatly stiffen the resistance of all other classes against any innovation, and to fix men's affections upon the good institutions handed down from an earlier generation (I, 200).

Turning to the leisure class itself, Veblen asked, why should it be conservative? To ask the question is to answer it:

The leisure class is in great measure sheltered from the stress of those economic exigencies which prevail in any modern, highly organized industrial community. The exigencies of the struggle for the means of life are less exacting for this class than for any other; and as a consequence of this privileged position we should expect to find it one of the least responsive of the classes of society to the demands which the situation makes for a further growth of institutions and a readjustment to an altered industrial situation. . . . The office of the leisure class in social evolution is to retard the movement and to conserve what is obsolescent (I, 198).

To put the matter colloquially, the leisure class resists change because it is the social class that "has it made." Situated in positions of wealth, status, and power, and owing all these to the social system as it stands, institutional alteration can scarcely improve, and is most likely to worsen, its position. It follows, Veblen concluded, that in general those who advocate social change by that act sacrifice identification with the leisure class.

Conservatism, being an upper-class characteristic, is decorous; and conversely, innovation, being a lower-class phenomenon, is vulgar. The first and most unreflected element in that instinctive revulsion and reprobation with which we turn from all social innovators is this sense of the essential vulgarity of the thing. . . . Innovation is bad form (I, 200).

The foregoing discussion covers the central core of *The Theory of the Leisure Class,* although it does not exhaust all the ideas contained in that study. Neither does it completely reveal the larger foundations of Veblen's viewpoint, nor the reservations and the elaborations contained in this first book, and in later books and essays. Much of this more extended discussion will be attempted in subsequent chapters; some will be considered here.

The starting point in Veblen's thought is that human behavior is a product of two major elements: man as an animal and man in society. Conflict, ever present in man and in society, is an integral and ubiquitous part of Veblen's analyses. Within man himself there is constant warfare between constructive and destructive "instincts."* This conflict is both a reflection and a determinant of similar tension in society. The result is continuous social change, for better or for worse, emanating from man's struggle within himself and the struggle between men organized into contending groups of various kinds (nations, classes, etc.)

The aim of this struggle—survival, welfare, status, dominance, achievement—is congruent with its source; the outcome is unpredictable, a matter of "opaque cause and effect" or "blind drift." Veblen saw social evolution in effect as a race between the life-giving and the life-destroying— between the cooperative and the predatory—elements in man and society. In man the chief life-giving factors are what

---

* The term "instinct" as used by Veblen has led to much confusion and unwarranted criticism. How he meant the term will be clarified below, pp. —. It will be seen that Veblen was considerably clearer in his use of words than were his hastier critics.

Veblen called the parental bent, the instinct of workmanship and the instinct of idle curiosity.

The parental bent is the source of habitual efforts to provide for the future of the species, and it is closely linked to the instinct of workmanship, which inclines man to seek quality and efficiency in production. Standing off to the side is the instinct of idle curiosity, the fount of learning and science, only indirectly related to production. Taken together, these account for the educational and cultural achievements of the past, its technological progress, and workmanlike production—in a word, they account for the increasingly comfortable survival of the species.

The destructive elements in man and in society Veblen found in what most would view as ideological verities and laudable institutional bulwarks. What is commonly termed individual enterprise, Veblen called "self-help," and he saw this aspect of economic activity as motivated by essentially predatory considerations, and as succeeding at the expense of the community. Around this notion he erected much of his *Theory of Business Enterprise*, in which he viewed the activities of businessmen as acquisitive rather than productive, the aim of which was "to get something for nothing"; the consequences of these same activities were those of "industrial sabotage," inefficiency, and "sand in the gears."

Veblen's attitude toward other major institutions of organized society—e.g., the state, patriotism, the military, organized religion—was not less scathing. These latter he saw as the repositories of "force and fraud" (while not neglecting the role of fraud in business enterprise, as embodied in salesmanship). For those who do not offend easily, Veblen's long note comparing religion and salesmanship (X, 319-25), still stands as one of the brightest social satires in American literature. His view of the church may be sensed from his statement that the pulpit is "the accredited vent for the exudation of effete matter from the cultural organism" (VIII, 53).

Like the constructive institutions in society, the state, religion and warfare are linked to basic inclinations in man, to destructive "instincts." Most simply, the destructive instincts Veblen classified as "exploitative," or "sportsman-like." Veblen's use of the word "sport" is, for those in our culture, ironic, designed to jar those who think in terms of "good sports," and of the graces of competitive athletic displays. For Veblen, athletic activity had its social roots in the predatory activities of warrior and hunter; its most meaningful contemporary explanation lay in the degree to which participation in organized athletics, by its exhibition of wasteful prowess, was a mark of leisure-class membership. Veblen was by no means disinterested in physical fitness; but he argued, for example, that "the relation of football to physical culture is much the same as that of the bull-fight to agriculture" (I, 261).

The "instinct of sportsmanship," then, or the "exploitative instinct," is a predatory inclination, setting man against man in a relationship of parasitism. This must be compared with the constructive "instincts" which are cooperative in their general implications. The state, the military and the church are all buttressed by the predatory instincts, with patriotism and religious belief acting to preserve the existing order—by diverting attention from the matter-of-fact through excitation or "make-believe."

Veblen lumped the enterprises and the individuals directing and manning business enterprise, the state, the military, and the church into one category: the vested interests. He saw them as a group which consciously or not combined to extract a toll—in the fashion of medieval robber barons—from the common man and, to make matters worse, set standards of consumption, behavior, and attitude virtually guaranteeing that the common man would find himself permanently in the thralldom of the status quo—or worse.

The status quo, in turn, Veblen saw as necessarily out of keeping with the everchanging needs of a healthy society. The status quo is but another name for the sum of social institutions at any time. With regard to such institutions,

the characteristic attitude of the [leisure] class may be summed up in the maxim: "Whatever is, is right"; whereas the law of natural selection, as applied to human institutions, gives the axiom: "Whatever is, is wrong." Not that the institutions of to-day are wholly wrong for the purposes of the life of to-day, but they are, always and in the nature of things, wrong to some extent. They are the result of a more or less inadequate adjustment of the methods of living to a situation which prevailed at some point in the past development; and they are therefore wrong by something more than the interval which separates the present situation from that of the past (I, 207).

It was one of Veblen's recurring arguments that the alternative to a movement toward economic and political democracy was not simply maintenance of the status quo; it was reversion to a barbaric state. This argument was hinted at in *The Theory of the Leisure Class*, developed more suggestively in *Imperial Germany and the Industrial Revolution* (1915), and made explicit in an extraordinarily insightful essay "The Opportunity of Japan" (1915; in XI, 248 ff.).

Veblen's values were those of a democrat, a pacifist, and a scientist. He abhorred concentrated power of any sort, social violence, and what he saw as the deadly grip of the irrational on men's minds and actions. His hopes for humanity rested on the constructive elements in man, and their reflections in science and technology. The latter could progress, he believed, only by the removal or periodic renovation of the institutions supporting "force and fraud": the vested interests in the military, organized religion, politics, and business.

The kind of man Veblen was—the things he praised or attacked, the developments he hoped for or feared, his intellectual capacities and inclinations—cannot be understood merely by looking at the world in which he lived. But Veblen's world—its problems, its achievements, its ideas—was nevertheless fundamental in shaping him.

Creative thinkers do not and cannot work in a vacuum, however original they may be. Veblen was much influenced, positively or negatively, by the leading thinkers of the nineteenth and early twentieth centuries. The most influential of these was undoubtedly Charles Darwin, whose theories of physical evolution Veblen modified and applied to the process of social change.

> The life of man in society, just like the life of other species, is a struggle for existence, and therefore it is a process of selective adaptation. The evolution of social structure has been a process of natural selection of institutions. . . . The forces which have shaped the development of human life and of social structure are no doubt ultimately reducible to terms of living tissue and material environment; but proximately, for the purpose in hand, these forces may best be stated in terms of an environment, partly human, partly non-human, and a human subject with a more or less definite physical and intellectual constitution (I, 188-89).

Veblen was neither the first nor the last to adapt Darwinian notions to the process of social change; indeed, in the latter part of the nineteenth century there emerged a number of influential social scientists—Herbert Spencer in England, and William Graham Sumner in America, to mention the two most important—who have come to be called "Social Darwinians."* But the adaptations of Darwin by this school of thought, in Veblen's view, were seriously and fundamentally in error. The Social Darwinians applied the concept of "survival of the fittest" to economic behavior by pointing to those whose accumulation of wealth was greatest and calling them the "fittest." In addition, Spencer and Sumner erected the evolutionary point of view into a rationale for laissez-faire economics.

Apart from the fact that Veblen did not accept the idea of "the survival of the fittest" in its vulgar connotation, his whole concept of *what* was evolving differed from that of the Social Darwinians. It was the evolution of *social institutions* that occupied Veblen's attention; that, and the importance

---

* See Richard Hofstadter, *Social Darwinism in American Thought* (Boston: The Beacon Press, 1955), for a comprehensive discussion and analysis of this development, and of Veblen's critical relationship to it.

of the nature and evolution of social institutions in providing an understanding of the process of social change. Far from seeing the ruling members of society as examples of the highest form of *human* development, Veblen looked upon their role in society as essentially atavistic, as echoes and holdovers of an earlier, barbaric society. Social progress for Veblen depended upon the harmonizing of the machine technology with appropriate institutional developments. This was doubtless a value judgment by Veblen—something he pretended to eschew—but whatever may be said on that score, it set him at the other end of the pole from the Social Darwinians.

Veblen was also much influenced by the psychologist Jacques Loeb, by William James, and by John Dewey. But, next to Darwin, the greatest—not entirely positive—influence on Veblen was probably that of Karl Marx. Veblen's analysis of Marxian thought was severely critical, and in some instances devastatingly so; but if Veblen was critical of Marx for his metaphysical and teleological bent, for his optimistic assumptions about the place of reason and human volition in determining the rate and direction of social change, and for paying too little attention to the diversities among and between societies, still he appreciated Marx's insistence on class struggle, the importance of technology as a prime mover in social change, and Marx's analysis of the underlying factors making for persistent tendencies toward monopoly and depression in capitalist economies.

In Veblen's hands, Marxian ideas were sometimes softened and sometimes hardened; always they were transmuted by the particular quality of Veblen's viewpoint, affected by his time and place.

What Veblen named as the vested interests, Marx called the ruling class; Veblen's underlying population was Marx's proletariat. However, where Marx saw the proletariat ultimately rising up to overthrow the ruling class, Veblen saw it as emulating the vested interests, as seeking to be like them. Veblen had a substantially greater respect for the hold of the irrational and the traditional on the common man than did Marx, and it was this distinction—owed in large part to the different times and places in which they wrote and lived —that made Veblen a pessimist and Marx an optimist.

Like most of his contemporaries, Marx (1818-1883) accepted the ideas of progress and rationality. He expected rational behavior on the part of both the capitalist and working classes, and he assumed that the long-run outcome of their conflict with each other, given the steady improvement of technology, would be the triumph of what Marx thought of as a rational form of social organization: socialism.

Veblen reached intellectual maturity almost half a century after Marx. Much had changed in that period. Consequently, Veblen had less need to speculate on, and more opportunity to observe, the impact of industrialism. In addition, Veblen wrote when philosophical speculation in social studies was beginning to give way to empirical study. Thus armed and inclined, Veblen looked about him and saw a working class that in values and motivation was scarcely different from its masters. He saw a working class that, far from wishing to abolish the economic system under which it worked, sought largely to occupy a more rewarding and honorific role within it. In short, he saw emulation, not revolutionary agitation, as the most persistent motive force of the working class.

There is . . . no warrant in the Darwinian scheme of things for asserting *a priori* that the class interest of the working class will bring them to take a stand against the propertied class. It may as well be that their training in subservience to their employers will bring them again to realize the equity and excellence of the established system of subjection and unequal distribution of wealth. . . . It may be that the working classes will go forward along the line of the socialistic ideals and enforce a new deal, in which there shall be no economic class discrepancies, no international animosity, no dynastic politics. . . . It is quite impossible on Darwinian ground to foretell whether the "proletariat" will go on to establish the socialistic revolution or turn aside again, and sink their force in the broad sands of patriotism. It is a question of habit and native propensity and of the

range of stimuli to which the proletariat are exposed
and are to be exposed, and what may be the outcome
is not a matter of logical consistency, but of response to
stimulus (VIII, 441-42).

Although Veblen had a high regard for Marx as an economist—"there is no system of economic theory more logical
than that of Marx" (VIII, 410-11)—he viewed him as a
"romantic philosopher"; one whose analysis of social change
was colored by his hopes, and which at critical stages departed from an analysis of "opaque cause and effect."
Veblen was not innocent of such departures himself, but
aside from the persistent reliance he placed on the instinct
of workmanship, Veblen only sporadically allowed wish to
take the place of thought. In the opening pages of *The Instinct of Workmanship* (1914) Veblen recognized that the
term "instinct" was "no longer well seen among students of
those biological sciences where [it] once had a great vogue"
(III, 1-2). But he goes on to say that

a genetic inquiry into institutions will address itself to
the growth of habits and conventions, as conditioned by
the material environment and by the innate and persistent propensities of human nature; and for these propensities, as they take effect in the give and take of
cultural growth, no better designation than the time-
worn "instinct" is available (III, 2-3).

Veblen provides a clear and unequivocal statement of
what he means by "instinct":

As the term is here used, therefore, and indeed as it
is currently understood, the instincts are to be defined
or described neither in mechanical terms of those ana-
tomical or physiological aptitudes that causally underlie
them or that come into action in the functioning of any
given instinct, nor in terms of the movements of orientation or taxis involved in the functioning of each. The
distinctive feature by the mark of which any given in-

stinct is identified is to be found in the particular character of the purpose to which it drives. "Instinct," as
contradistinguished from tropismatic action, involves
consciousness and adaptation to an end aimed at (III,
4).

He goes on to say that

"instinct" . . . denotes the conscious pursuit of an objective end which the instinct in question makes worth
while. . . . The ends of life, then, the purposes to be
achieved, are assigned by man's instinctive proclivities;
but the ways and means of accomplishing those things
which the instinctive proclivities so make worth while
are a matter of intelligence. . . . Men take thought, but
the human spirit, that is to say the racial endowment
of instinctive proclivities, decides what they shall take
thought of, and how and to what effect (III, 5-6).

Veblen did not use the term "instinct" to refer to what are
popularly thought of as unthinking reactions. These he
termed "tropismatic." Where his critics have accused Veblen
of a lack of sophistication in his use of the term "instinct,"
they have carelessly assumed that he meant *tropisms* rather
than *propensities;* or, perhaps more usually, they have dissented from his consistent view of man as an animal. Such a
view did not cause Veblen to overlook the special intelligence
of man, nor the role of this in the evolution of instinctive behavior. Thus,

all instinctive behavior is subject to development and
hence to modification by habit. Such impulsive action
as is in no degree intelligent, and so suffers no adaptation through habitual use, is not properly to be called
instinctive; it is rather to be classed as tropismatic. In
human conduct the effects of habit in this respect are
particularly far-reaching. In man the instincts appoint
less of a determinate sequence of action, and so leave

a more open field for adaptation of behavior to the circumstances of the case (III, 38).

In short, Veblen used the term "instinct" to cover much of what is loosely called "human nature." The area of thought and behavior thus referred to would include the values and ingrained habits of man, both of which are subject to change, but only slowly and under substantial stress.

The instinct of workmanship is linked closely to what Veblen called the parental bent. The nature of the link, in his view, is that "the instinct of workmanship is in the main a propensity to work out the ends which the parental bent makes worth while" (III, 48). And the parental bent is "an ever resilient solicitude for the welfare of the young and the prospective fortunes of the group" (III, 48). Thus, the parental bent leads men to take eye to the future, as regards the factors making for well-being. The instinct of workmanship is concerned with the here and now, with the factors making for efficiency, workmanlike standards, "and getting the next job done."

All this would seem to stand in sharp contrast with Veblen's strictures on the "conventional antipathy to useful effort." The apparent contradiction Veblen resolves by pointing out that although the instinct of workmanship and the parental bent taken together have been fundamental in preserving the species,

man's great advantage over other species in the struggle for survival has been his superior facility in turning the forces of his environment to account . . . , [to which] he owes his position as lord of creation. It is not a proclivity to effort, but to achievement—to the compassing of an end. His primacy is in the last resort an industrial or economic primacy (XI, 80-81).

It is quite possible, Veblen concludes, for men to engage in conspicuous waste, consumption, and leisure, and impress (or attempt to impress) others with their leisure class status, while simultaneously bending to the instinct of workmanship.

But in order to do both, the actor must convince himself that what he does is worthwhile. Thus,

> the popular reprobation of waste goes to say that in order to be at peace with himself the common man must be able to see in any and all human effort and human enjoyment an enhancement of life and well-being on the whole. In order to meet with unqualified approval, any economic fact must approve itself under the test of impersonal usefulness—usefulness as seen from the point of view of the generically human (I, 98).

Veblen's evolutionary views prompted him to the notion that "in the beginning" man must have been a workmanlike and "substantially a peaceful animal" in order to survive. He looked upon the predatory life of man as following upon his successful attempts to cope with the economics of survival in the prehistoric past. Consequently, he saw man's "basic" nature as dependent upon "an aptitude for avoiding direct conflict" and upon his facility in devising tools and coping with nature. Thus, waste must be dignified with rhetoric; war justified by "some colorable motive of another kind."

> What meets unreserved approval is such conduct as furthers human life on the whole, rather than such as furthers the invidious or predatory interest of one as against another (XI, 84).

Saying all this and more, Veblen held little hope that the "basic" qualities of man would assert themselves, largely because man's economic progress had been so great that he could survive while "playing fast and loose" with the fundamental conditions of survival in the process of natural selection. The contrast and balance between Veblen's infrequent optimism and his deep pessimism are well exemplified in an oft-quoted passage:

> In the cases where it has happened that those instincts which make directly for the material welfare of the com-

munity, such as the parental bent and the sense of
workmanship, have been present in such potent force,
or where the institutional elements at variance with the
continued life-interests of the community of the civilization in question have been in a sufficiently infirm state,
there the bonds of custom, prescription, principles, prec-
edent, have been broken—or loosened or shifted so as
to let the current of life and cultural growth go on, with
or without substantial retardation. But history records
more frequent and more spectacular instances of the
triumph of imbecile institutions over life and culture
than of peoples who have by force of instinctive insight
saved themselves alive out of a desperately precarious
institutional situation, such, for instance, as now faces
the people of Christendom (III, 25).

Whatever glimmers of hope Veblen may have detected in
the "constructive instincts" at one time, he had abandoned
by 1923, when he wrote his last book (*Absentee Ownership*).
When he died—in 1929, on the edge of a series of economic,
political, and military catastrophes whose end is not yet in
sight—Veblen was profoundly, unrelievedly pessimistic.

Chapter 2

VEBLEN AND AMERICAN CAPITALISM

Veblen probed far and wide, but his most persistent focus was American society. The American economy is the subject of *The Theory of Business Enterprise* (1904), despite Veblen's prefatory statement that he is inquiring "into the nature, causes, utility, and further drift of business enterprise" (II, v), without geographical qualification. Almost all the contemporary illustrations and argumentation are drawn from the American situation of Veblen's day. In *Absentee Ownership and Business Enterprise in Recent Times* (1923), the American focus is explicit (the subtitle is "The Case of America"). *Absentee Ownership* differs from the earlier book in two major respects, neither fundamental to Veblen's analysis of American capitalism: 1) it is less abstract, and more up to date than the *Theory;* 2) the mood is more openly critical. Here we shall draw largely upon the earlier book for the essence of Veblen's analysis of American capitalism; in a later chapter the more concrete materials of *Absentee Ownership* will be examined.

Veblen had good reason to keep America in mind as he attempted a theory of business enterprise. He aimed to lay bare the inner logic and basic workings of the system of industrial capitalism. Although industrial capitalism first came to exist in Britain, it had developed, he believed, further and in a "purer" state in America—relatively uninfluenced by the historical constraints of dynastic politics, the social controls, and the military adventures characteristic of the transatlantic countries.

In studying business enterprise, Veblen centered his focus upon the changing nature of economic institutions. The process of change itself was for Veblen the result of continuous interaction between 1) the aims and methods of business enterprise, and 2) the logic of industrial technology. Because the principles of business enterprise and the spread of industrialism were so pervasive in America, Veblen could use America as a "model" for a general analysis of industrial capitalism. For him, the two great systems of capitalism and industrialism dominating America had in some respects a complementary relationship; but the eventual relationship was one of conflict and irreconcilability. His conclusions can be stated as follows: either the industrial technology would lead capitalism to be superseded by a qualitatively different society, involving, e.g., social control and planning; or, to prevent that, the modern capitalist system would be forced to turn to a totalitarian system of control—à la Nazi Germany—of which business enterprise would itself ultimately become a victim. In both cases, Veblen took centralized control, or at least coordination, to be an inescapable accompaniment of modern industrialism. The question is simply: control by whom, and to what ends?

Like Marx—but with a different theory and with somewhat gloomier expectations—Veblen saw capitalism as hastening the spread of a technological system whose institutional needs and implications could not permanently coexist. Fundamental to this theory were Veblen's views on both the nature of business enterprise and of industrial technology.

Veblen was not an economic determinist; he was insistent about the role of "non-economic" factors in affecting the pace and direction of social change. But the basis for any understanding of Western civilization was, for Veblen, its economy. "To a greater extent than any other known phase of culture, modern Christendom takes its complexion from its economic organization. . . . Its characteristic features, and at the same time the forces by virtue of which it dominates modern culture, are the machine process and investment for profit" (II, 1).

And again, "Business enterprise and the machine process are the two prime movers in modern culture" (II, 377).

Like Adam Smith, and most subsequent economists, Veblen took for granted that the economic well-being of a capitalist society is a by-product, not the intended result, of the businessman's attempt to make profits. For Smith, and his successors, the alchemy that transformed individual self-seeking into *social* gain was "the invisible hand" of competition in the market. Veblen accepted this view of the businessman as bent on gain. He departed from the conventional view in pursuing Smith's dichotomy to its logical conclusion. Out of this emerged one of Veblen's basic concepts, the distinction between "business" and "industry." Business is a means of making money; industry is a matter of making goods. And, "work that is, on the whole, useless or detrimental to the community at large may be as gainful to the businessman and to the workmen whom he employs as work that contributes substantially to the aggregate livelihood" (II, 63).

What was benign in Smith became deadly in Veblen.

But Veblen did not object to, or depart from, Smith's analysis, as such. He had a high regard for Adam Smith, but he could not see how a set of principles developed to accord with the needs and possibilities of the eighteenth century could fit harmoniously with the drastically changed world of production, business, politics and culture over a century later.

The principles of business enterprise were founded on and made workable by a set of preconceptions and assumptions in the eighteenth century which, in terms of scope, and when compared to those of the twentieth century, were as the hummingbird to the eagle. The philosophical expression of these principles was based upon the concept of natural rights; and the institutional application of the natural rights philosophy—in law, in government, in economic affairs—was essential to a freely working capitalist economy. Movement toward this goal was already pronounced in Smith's England; it reached its fullest expression in the America of Veblen's young manhood.

In this context, according to Veblen,

Natural rights, as they found their way into law and equity, were in effect the assumed equal rights of men so situated on a plane of at least constructive equality that the individuals concerned would be left in a position of effectively free choice if conventional restrictions were done away (II, 271).

Furthermore, he continued,

The movement of opinion on natural-rights ground converged to an insistence on the system of natural liberty, so called. But this insistence on natural liberty did not contemplate the abrogation of all conventional prescription. 'The simple and obvious system of natural liberty' [as in Smith] meant freedom from restraint on any other prescriptive ground than that afforded by the rights of ownership. In its economic bearing the system of natural liberty meant a system of free pecuniary contract (II, 271-72).

We live at a time when modifications of "free pecuniary contract" (i.e., impingements on the right of property owners to use and profit from their property) are manifested with increasing frequency. Examples of this development may be found in tax and wage legislation, to mention only two of the innumerable instances that could be cited. But in the years when Veblen's ideas were forming, the natural rights philosophy in America was dominant and virtually unchallenged. As challenges were mounted in ensuing years, Veblen's ideas often served as one basis of attack.

While Veblen wrote, the center of the economic stage was being occupied by large-scale industry, continental and intercontinental transportation and marketing, and the modern corporation. To Veblen, these and other developments made of the "simple and obvious system of natural liberty" little more than the rhetorical sheep's clothing worn by the wolves of industrial capitalism. Granting that in Smith's day institutions founded on such a concept may have been conducive to economic advancement, Veblen demurred for his own time (not to mention subsequent years) when he pointed out that

> The scheme of natural rights grew up and found secure lodgement in the common sense of the community, as well as with its lawgivers and courts, under the discipline of the small industry and petty trade ("domestic industry") whose development culminated in the eighteenth century. In industrial matters the efficient and autonomous factor . . . was the individual workman, his personal force, dexterity, and diligence; similarly in the petty trade of the precapitalistic English situation the decisive factor was the discretion and sagacity of the small merchant and the petty employer, who stood in direct personal relations with their customers and their employees (II, 270).

Veblen thus points out that the abolition of customary and statutory economic regulation (one of Smith's primary aims) could, in that setting, make competition effective and beneficial. As industry expanded, and grew more impersonal and comprehensively organized, so too did a system designed for small-scale production become obsolete *de facto*—but not *de jure*.

Although those who know the economic history of eighteenth century England will find the picture of "small industry and petty trade" in certain respects overblown, Veblen's point is nonetheless well-taken, given the sharp contrast between the industrial organization of the eighteenth and the twentieth centuries.

Because of the change in technology that ensued after the eighteenth century, the size of the business firm, its work force, its product, its markets, and its problems and possibilities were all transformed. One need only contrast a Darby of Coalbrookdale—knowing his workmen, operating a family enterprise with his own capital, and with a limited product and geographical market—with a Carnegie. The latter turned out more iron and steel in a day than Darby did in a year; had numerous and far-flung plants, thousands of workmen, countless different products and extensive markets; and he financed his operations with "other people's money." To believe that a legal and social system fitted for Darby's world would suit Carnegie's would be akin, for Veblen, to believing that a tractor could run on oats.

Technological change has meant much more than greater efficiency in production. Among other things, it has caused the businessman to alter his methods. Thus,

> With a fuller development of the modern close-knit and comprehensive industrial system, the point of chief attention for the businessman has shifted from the old-fashioned surveillance and regulation of a given industrial process, with which his livelihood was once bound up, to an alert redistribution of investments from less to more gainful ventures, and to a strategic control of the conjunctures of business through shrewd investments and coalitions with other businessmen (II, 24-25).

Unlike most other economists, Veblen did not deplore the disappearance of competition through coalitions (i.e., through the consolidation of many previously competing firms into one or a few giant corporations). He held that numerous competitors in the same industry were incompatible with industrial efficiency. For Veblen, the notion that competition could be made to work by *fiat* (e.g., through antitrust laws) was sentimental. Consequently,

> . . . it is scarcely an overstatement to say that probably the largest, assuredly the securest and most unquestionable, service rendered by the great modern captains of industry is this curtailment [via consolidation] of the business to be done,—this sweeping retirement of businessmen as a class . . . , the definitive cancelment of opportunities for private enterprise . . . , [and] an avoidance of that systematic mutual hindrance that characterizes the competitive management of industry. To the community at large the work of pecuniary management,

it appears, is less serviceable the more there is of it
(II, 48).

Veblen's attitude toward the concentration of "enterprise"
can be easily misinterpreted if not related to his more general
analysis, particularly as regards industrial technology. In
Veblen's view, when an industry has reached a stage of
development (in terms of its technology and markets and
productive capacity) such that combination becomes desirable and feasible in business terms, the existence of numerous
"competitors" has already ceased to serve a beneficial *economic* function. Veblen did not expect benevolence or economic statesmanship from the resulting powerful corporations
—indeed, his *Theory of Business Enterprise* is based on pre-
cisely the opposite expectation. Nor, unlike most liberal
economists, did Veblen expect that much could be hoped for
in the way of governmental control. His theory of the state
told Veblen that those most deserving of control were for all
important purposes immune from state power; and the more
powerful the corporation, the greater the immunity.

Veblen did not assume businessmen's morality to be better
or worse than that of the average men in the community; the
aims and functions of businessmen, not their morality, were
his concern. Echoing Smith, Veblen argued that the injection
of social motivations into business affairs would "detract from
business efficiency, and an undue yielding to them on the part
of the businessman is to be deprecated as an infirmity" (II,
41). He did grant, however, that "a businessman will rather
use wool than shoddy, at the same price" (II, 42*n*).

Although Veblen claimed scientific detachment from the
matters he analyzed, there can be little doubt that he had an
aversion to businessmen, and to the business system. But the
force of his theory does not depend upon dislike of businessmen; it depends upon what Veblen considered the prime
function of an economy: *serviceability*. By this term, Veblen
meant the ongoing ability of an economy to produce goods
and services required for the health of the evolving *community* (I, 227). The concept of serviceability underlies
Veblen's basic distinction between industrial (productive)

and business (pecuniary) functions. The former contribute to the well-being of the community; the latter contribute to the wealth of one part of the community, often at the expense of the remainder. From this standpoint, business principles are incompatible with the technology of modern industry.*

In 1904, when Veblen first began to analyze the technology of his time, industry was still dominated by *mechanical* processes. Chemistry and electrification—not to mention the electronic achievements of the present—had only recently gained importance. This limited progress makes Veblen's analysis all the more remarkable. Despite the important technological achievements of the past half-century or so, Veblen's characterization of the nature and implications of industrial technology remains valid—it has, if anything, even greater force than in his own time.

Veblen's starting point for an understanding of modern technology is succinctly stated: ". . . the modern industrial system at large bears the character of a comprehensive, balanced, mechanical process" (II, 16). Such a system, or any producing plant within it, will be efficient and profitable to the degree that it *combines* the following characteristics: 1) the product is standardized; 2) production is automatic and continuous; 3) plant is large-scale. These in turn require and imply basic characteristics for the economy within which a given plant operates: 4) transportation, communications, and marketing facilities are large-scale, cheap, and coordinated; 5) the production of a given good (e.g., steel) is synchronized with goods produced "behind and ahead" of it (e.g., respectively, coal and automobiles); 6) the firm has access to large amounts of capital, and a disciplined labor force; 7) consumers and industry are able and willing to absorb large and continuous (and rising) quantities of standardized products.

---

* It is one of the more intriguing characteristics of economic thought since Veblen that both his view of business principles and his interpretation of the logic of industrial technology are generally accepted by economists. However, with a few notable exceptions— John Maurice Clark, e.g.—most economists continue to work within a theoretical framework that sets aside these ideas.

Putting all these and lesser characteristics together yields, in Veblen's words, a system at once well-knit, interlocking, and, of necessity, one in which massiveness and standardization march hand in hand with a high degree of interdependence—for business firms, workers, and the society at large. This state was already apparent to Veblen in 1904; today it is even more apparent that a society reaping the economic benefits of industrial technology pays for its prosperity in the coin of a precarious interdependence, inscribed with the symbol of mass man.

Mature industrialism, and all that it connotes and requires in the way of order and balance, has no room in it for the pleasant anarchy of the "simple and obvious system of natural liberty," nor can industrialism function with laws, institutions, and economics assuming such simplicity. Veblen noted that, whatever businessmen might say, they did not live by such a system of atomistic individualism. Each year of technological advance brought with it a further "concatenation of industrial processes," and increasing interdependence between and among the separate branches and sectors of the economy.

Such developments did not lead to any relaxation of the pride of place given to natural (i.e. "property") rights. But because the costs of economic disturbance (by which Veblen meant speculative and cyclical fluctuations) rose in geometric proportion as industrialization proceeded, steps had to be taken that would mitigate, or at least insulate the business firm from, such disturbances. In Veblen's view this necessary revision of strategy in no sense implied a growth of feelings of social responsibility among businessmen. It meant simply that self-interest dictated new methods. One principal outcome was the consolidation movement raging in Veblen's day.

Modern circumstances do not permit the competitive management of property invested in industrial enterprise, much less its management in detail by individual owners. In short, the exercise of free contract, and the other powers inhering in the natural right of ownership, are incompatible with the modern machine technology.

Business discretion necessarily centers in other hands than those of the general body of owners [who are] necessarily reduced to the practical status of pensioners dependent on the discretion of the great holders of immaterial wealth; the general body of businessmen are similarly . . . disfranchised in point of business initiative and reduced to a bureaucratic hierarchy under the same guidance; and the rest, the populace, is very difficult to bring into the schedule except as raw material of industry (II, 266-67).

The guiding agent of industrialization in its youthful and most energetic phase in America (1830-1880) was the "captain of industry." By this term, Veblen referred to the hard-driving businessman who ran his firm at first hand either as a proprietorship or a partnership—managing, raising capital, knowing his work force, often as much an engineer as a businessman. By the 1880's the "captain of industry" had already begun to give way to the "captain of finance"; the proprietorship to the corporation.*

The economics of industry accordingly moved from competition and the search for lower costs to pools and gentlemen's agreements, and thence to mergers and effectively restricted production. The shift from control by an impersonal market to controlled markets, from competition to collusion and monopoly, became desirable and even necessary to business, as productive capacity sporadically grew more rapidly than demand—resulting in periods of intense competition, forcing prices down to and even below costs.

The first major waves of mergers in the United States took

---

* In Veblen's later writings, he was to substitute "absentee ownership" for "business enterprise," and the "captain of solvency" for the "captain of finance." By absentee ownership, Veblen meant a situation—which he took to be typical by the 1920's—where those with claims on production derived from ownership rights controlled (directly, or through managers), but made no contribution to, production, and bore only a predatory relationship to the productive process. The captain of solvency was the captain of finance writ large, with the holding company instead of the corporation, and interlocks between industrial and financial institutions as the dynamic core of the economy.

place in the years immediately preceding the publication of the *Theory*. In the space of a few years industrial, public utility, and transportation trusts numbering 445 were formed. They represented consolidations of over 8,500 originally independent companies. The United States Steel Corporation, for example, with a capitalization of one billion dollars, was formed in 1901 from eleven corporations, owning 785 operating plants. Little wonder that Veblen took the corporation as the "representative firm," and that he saw its techniques as something other than beneficially competitive. The greater wonder (as we shall see in Chapter 3) is that Veblen's economist colleagues, in the midst of all this, continued to spin placid theories assuming a world that, if it had ever existed, did not exist in America or anywhere else as the twentieth century opened.

As the corporation became the key institution of the economy, the aims and practices of corporation finance became the key determinant of the economy's functioning. As Veblen wrote the *Theory*, this characteristic of the economy was only newly-emergent—"an inchoate growth of the immediate present [rather] than an accomplished fact of even the recent past" (II, 90). He was consciously tentative in his judgment of this development, and he was to shift his emphasis in the twenty years that elapsed between the *Theory* and *Absentee Ownership*. However, although the emphasis shifted, in a manner to be noted below, his judgment on the role of the corporation became not less but more critical.

In 1904, Veblen concentrated on two characteristics of the world of corporation finance, both stemming from the aim to gain a profit from investment, rather than from production; both turning on the role of the capitalized value of corporate assets—i.e., the value established on the basis of the expected earning power of present assets. The first of these two characteristics, and much the lesser in importance as Veblen saw it, was the role of the corporate "insider." What enlightened opinion then and later saw as the principal abuse of corporate finance, Veblen took as a normal feature: namely, the uses to which inside information could be put in the making of profits in the securities market. For expected earning-capacity

> as it takes shape in the surmises of outside investors,
> may differ appreciably from the actual earning-capacity
> of the capital as it is known to its managers, and it may
> readily be to the latter's interest that such a discrepancy
> between actual and imputed earning-capacity should
> arise (II, 155).

The rôle of inside information in fortune-making was considerable in Veblen's day, and was to remain so until the reforms of the New Deal in the thirties. If behavior based on inside information has not completely disappeared even now, it has nonetheless lost its earlier significance. In the *Theory,* and even more so in *Absentee Ownership,* Veblen relegated the "insider" problem to a subordinate position in his analysis of the nature and meaning of the corporation as the dominant institution of the American economy.

For Veblen, the strategic meaning of the corporation and of corporation finance had to do with its relationship to pricing, the distribution of income, and the relationship between these and the overall performance of the economy. In the next chapter we shall examine Veblen's criticisms of conventional economics, which were directed largely at its assumptions. However, given the assumptions of conventional economics, this much can be said: in a world of effective market competition, prices would be kept down to the level where costs* would be met—on the average, and over time, neither excess profits nor losses would be made by the firms in the industry—and the amount produced by the industry would accord with the demands of the community for that product in combination with the range of other products available and the income needed to clear the market and

---

* Where "costs" includes a "normal" return to invested capital, and "normal" means that return sufficient to attract and keep the desired amount of productive capacity in the industry, and where "desired amount" is defined in terms of demand and supply conditions in all other industries as they relate to the one under consideration.

maximize consumer satisfaction. Demand and supply operating in such an impersonal market would bring about "optimum" cost and optimum production and an optimum allocation of scarce resources. Such would be the economy hoped for by Adam Smith, but it has seldom existed outside textbooks.

In the corporate world that Veblen saw about him in 1904 (and still more so, in that of the twenties), prices were set by corporations, not established in an impersonal, competitive market:

"Cutthroat" competition, that is to say, free competitive selling, can be done away by "pooling the interests" of the competitors, so soon as all or an effective majority of the business concerns which are rivals in the market combine and place their business management under one directive head. When this is done, by whatever method, selling of goods or services at competitively varying prices is replaced by collective selling . . . at prices fixed on the basis of "what the traffic will bear." That is to say, prices are fixed by consideration of what scale of prices will bring the largest aggregate net earnings, due regard being had to the effect of a lower price in increasing sales as well as to the reduction of cost through the increase of output (II, 258).

In Veblen's analysis, the "largest aggregate net earnings" soon becomes the "reasonable" rate of profit on investment. But this is a rate of return to assets that tend over time to be overcapitalized—as capacity increases and technology improves (reducing costs) more rapidly than the market can absorb the increased production. In order to maintain reasonable profits, prices have to be set at levels that, in the absence of comprehensive and interlocked monopolies, cannot generally be maintained. Put briefly, assets are valued in periods of optimism. When the future does not maintain the conditions that produced the optimism, prices are established that —combining collusive pricing with restricted production— attempt to achieve by market control what was earlier a product of economic buoyancy. One conclusion Veblen drew from this set of relationships bears on his theory of depression and provides a link between corporation finance, investment, consumption, and employment:

> The great coalitions and business manoeuvres connected with them have the effect of adding to the large fortunes of the greater businessmen; which adds to the large incomes that cannot be spent in consumptive expenditures; which accelerates the increase of investments; which brings competition if there is a chance for it; which tends to bring on depression. . . . The great coalitions, therefore, seem to carry the seed of this malady of competition, and this evil consequence can accordingly be avoided only on the basis of so comprehensive and rigorous a coalition of business concerns as shall wholly exclude competition, even in the face of any conceivable amount of new capital seeking investment (II, 263-64).

In the course of periodic depressions, Veblen asserted, the problem would be exacerbated, for new firms would come into existence that would employ the most modern technology, put in place at low costs and low interest rates. They would function profitably, gradually inflate their capitalizations, and subsequently join their older (remaining) fellows to bring on the next depression.

Having allowed our discussion of the corporation to carry us over into Veblen's analysis of depression, let us pause a moment before continuing, and summarize the general lines along which his *Theory of Business Enterprise* moved. Veblen's view of the driving force of industrialism led him to anticipate, as social and political consequences, the worlds later to be painted by Huxley in *Brave New World*, and Orwell in *1984*, as well as the business sociology analyzed by Whyte in *Organization Man*. In economics proper, Veblen anticipated by thirty years the discovery of the separation of corporate ownership and control, and the domination of the American economy by a few hundred giant corporations, posited by Berle and Means in their *Modern Corporation and Private Property.* But Veblen did not confine his attention to just these consequences of industrial capitalism—i.e., drives toward corporate concentration and market control, and the standardization of man. Of the many other processes taking their momentum from the operations of industrial capitalism—e.g., in the realm of education, news media, religion, and politics—the two most requiring comment here are concerned with 1) the persistent tendency of the economy toward depression, and 2) the impact of industrial capitalism on the working class and the resulting "social problem."

In Veblen's theory, the three major products of industrial capitalism—concentrated economic power, pervasive depressions, and labor unrest—combine to promote a fourth tendency. This last, the tendency for patriotism and militarism to be encouraged by business politics—what Veblen called "exercises in national integrity"—deflects the energies and aspirations that constitute the "social problem" into non-economic channels. That this conquest of the social problem must ultimately damage those who acquiesce in or encourage it constitutes the essence of Veblen's ironic view of the prospects for industrial capitalism.

The importance of this aspect of Veblen's analysis requires an extended discussion. The four elements of his position interlock: business principles and the machine process interact to produce concentrated economic power and persistent excess capacity; business power and its command over national politics enable it to quell labor unrest by diverting attention to questions of national pride and power; excess capacity is utilized, profitably, in unproductive consumption and waste, centering on a large and well-armed military establishment. To appreciate this argument, we must first examine the reasons for excess capacity and the relationship between this and depression.

Veblen's explanation of business crisis (i.e., depression) rests on the relationship between technological change and productivity, capitalization, prices, and profit expectations. Veblen's terminology is in some respects unique, but his analysis is remarkably close to the contemporary income theory based on Keynes's *General Theory of Employment, Interest and Money* (1936).

Veblen's starting point was his familiar distinction between "industry" and "business," and his strategic factor was profit expectations.

Since industry waits upon business, it is a matter of course that industrial depression is primarily a depression in business. But business is the quest of profits, and an inhibition of this quest must touch the seat of its vital motives. Industrial depression means that the businessmen engaged do not see their way to derive a satisfactory gain from letting the industrial process go forward on the lines and in the volume for which the material equipment of industry is designed (II, 213).

Under what circumstances would business firms "not see their way"? Veblen's answer is when there is "overproduction," which he immediately defines as excessive competition and unsatisfactory prices at healthy levels of production—i.e., as an inadequate level of effective demand.

There is an excess of goods, or of the means of producing them, above what is expedient on pecuniary grounds,—above what there is an effective demand for at prices that will repay the cost of production of the goods and leave something appreciable over as a profit. It is a question of prices and earnings. . . . There is too large a productive capacity; there are too many competitive producers and too much industrial apparatus to supply the market at reasonable prices. The matter reduces itself to a question of fair prices and ordinary profits (II, 216-17).

Like Keynes, Veblen utilized a theory of "effective demand," but with a different emphasis. For Veblen, the tendency for productive capacity to become "too large," with a resulting downward pressure on prices and profits, was an outcome of the unplanned and uncoordinated manner in which productive capacity grew, and the inability of the public to absorb the "inordinate productivity" of modern industry. His analysis relates profit expectations to the structure of supply and demand, and to the process that produces imbalance. As in contemporary income theory, if with a more sardonic terminology,

the explanation here offered of depression makes it a malady of the affections. The discrepancy which discourages businessmen is a discrepancy between that nominal capitalization which they have set their hearts upon through habituation in the immediate past and that actual capitalization value of their property which its current earning-capacity will warrant (II, 237).

Veblen, like Keynes, focussed on profit expectations. Unlike those who theorize within the Keynesian framework, Veblen integrated the structure and functioning of the business system (the province of "micro-economics") with the cyclical and growth performance of the economy (the province of "macro-economics")—an overall approach only now beginning to capture the interest of economists concerned with the low growth rate of the American economy.

On the other hand, Veblen failed to develop an adequate theory of consumption and investment, the strongest feature of the modern theory of employment. Put differently, Veblen did not systematically examine the reasons why new investment takes place; he asked only why restriction of production from existing investment goods occurs. Also, Veblen paid little explicit attention to consumption. For his analytical purposes, the capital-goods industries "show the modern industrial and business traits in an accentuated form and force, and they are, by consequence, in a strategically primary position in the business situation" (II, 181n). In Veblen's time this was a more reasonable position to take than it is today, because of the lesser role played then by consumer goods (e.g., in the years surrounding 1904, capital-goods production was expanding at just twice the rate of consumer-goods production).*

It is interesting to note that Veblen, Keynes, and Marx were alike in viewing the return to capital (profits) as the obvious aim of business investment; that, for all three, profits showed a tendency toward zero in the long run as the supply of capital, i.e., of productive capacity, increased. Again, for all three, this would be true only in the absence of compensating factors making for contrived or natural scarcities of goods—e.g., wars, technological revolutions, geographic expansion, monopolistic restriction of production.

Despite Veblen's incomplete theory of depression, he understood well the kinds of actions that could be used to offset depression. He specified these as a prophet of gloom, not as an advocate of reform. Like Keynes, he knew that stimuli to demand from whatever source—arms, pyramid building, dams and roads, digging holes and filling them up again, senseless consumption, for example—buoy the economy, create employment and maintain profitability.** What Keynes advocated, however, Veblen predicted, and his predictions were on the grim side. Why this was so for Veblen brings us back to the "fourth" development referred to earlier: namely, the relationship between depression, labor unrest, and the "social problem."

Veblen did not accept the Marxian theory of class struggle. But he did view labor's interests and outlook as being in substantial conflict with the system of business enterprise, because of the function of the industrial worker, and because of the latter's position at the bottom of the ladder of income and prestige in the economic system.

The sanctification of property rights contained in the natural-rights philosophy was, for the businessman, some

---

* It would seem clear that combining Veblen's analysis of structure and process with contemporary income theory and empirical investigation might go far toward improving our understanding of today's "macro" problems. This will be discussed in Chapter 5.

** One major difference is the weight Veblen gave to monopolistic restriction of production as a means of maintaining profits in the face of depression, a technique whose efficacy he probably overestimated.

combination of good sense and gospel truth. To the industrial worker, on the other hand, the same doctrine appeared as the practical expression of force and fraud: "force," because the legal framework prevented the worker from organizing in strength to improve his economic position;* "fraud," because the worker's daily, "matter-of-fact" association with industrial technology did not square with institutions assuming a handicraft technology. The "simple and obvious system of natural liberty," if it meant freedom to pursue profit for the employer, meant intermittent unemployment and coercion to the wage-earner. Veblen recognized the impulses behind the workers' felt needs to organize to improve their lot, but he argued that their success would be incompatible with the aims, institutions, and power of business enterprise.

> Industrial organization . . . rests on the distinction between business management and ownership. The workmen do not and cannot own or direct the industrial equipment and processes, so long as ownership prevails and industry is to be managed on business principles. The labor supply, or working population, can therefore not be included in the ideally complete business coalition . . . , however consummate the machine system and the business organization built upon it may become. So that when the last step in business coalition has been taken, there remains the competitive friction between the combined business capital and the combined workmen (II, 265-66).

Arriving at something like the same conclusion for somewhat different reasons, Marx predicted proletarian revolution and socialism as the outcome. Not so Veblen. Although he does not rule out this possibility, his emphasis is on the diversion of labor's energies and aims into irrational, noneconomic channels. Here business power and prestige, in a

---

* The National Labor Relations (Wagner) Act, the first generally meaningful step in improving the legal position of the worker was not passed until 1935.

business enterprise society, are vital elements in Veblen's theory. It is axiomatic for Veblen that in such a society—e.g., in America—political power and social prestige, as well as wealth, will be controlled by businessmen: "Representative government means, chiefly, representation of business interests" (II, 286).

Veblen does not put forth a crude theory of corruption, or of the naked use of power. He did not feel that either was necessary. In a society accepting the business system as natural, and therefore as desirable, it is equally natural that business criteria and practices will come to be taken for granted in all walks of life—in the schools, in the media of communication, in the courts, and in government.

It seldom happens, if at all, that the government of a civilized nation will persist in a course of action detrimental or not ostensibly subservient to the interests of the more conspicuous body of the community's businessmen (II, 287).

A conspiracy to this end is unnecessary, for

there is a naïve, unquestioning persuasion abroad among the body of the people to the effect that, in some occult way, the material interests of the populace coincide with the pecuniary interests of those businessmen who live within the scope of the same set of governmental contrivances (II, 286).

And corruption is beside the point. Referring to the tendency of the courts to find in favor of property holders, Veblen remarks:

In the nature of the case the owner alone has, ordinarily, any standing in court. All of which argues that there are probably very few courts that are in any degree corrupt or biased. . . . Efforts to corrupt them would be a work of supererogation, besides being immoral (II, 282*n*).

The bearing of all this on labor and the social problem is brought out by Veblen in the concluding chapter of the *Theory*, entitled "The Natural Decay of Business Enterprise."

And this is a question, not of what is conceivably, ideally, idyllically possible for the business community to do if they will take thought and act advisedly and concertedly toward a chosen cultural outcome, but of what is the probable cultural outcome to be achieved through business traffic carried on for business ends, not for cultural ends. It is a question not of what ought to be done, but what is to take place (II, 377). The question, therefore, remains, on the whole, a question of what businessmen may be expected to do for cultural growth on the motive of profits (II, 379).

Taking this question in the context of international rivalries for power and economic advantage (to be examined in Chapter 4), and given the disproportionate influence of businessmen on the press, on popular values, and in domestic politics, one major possibility is that businessmen would use their power to stimulate production through enlarged arms production and a large military establishment. In Veblen's eyes this possibility becomes a probability when the "corrective discipline" of applied patriotism is placed against the unrest of the laboring classes.

Veblen's view of the machine process as a promoter of institutional dissent by the industrial workers has been referred to before; what is also relevant are the propensities for emulation and conservatism in the working population, as they seek to become accepted and acceptable in a business society guided by leisure-class values. Emulation of leisure-class standards and the widespread propagation of those standards through advertising and the communications media promote conspicuous consumption, and in so doing simultaneously utilize productive capacity and deflect attention from persisting inequities. This process, taken together with the deep-seated inclination of man to display his prowess, joins business needs to produce a drift toward the garrison state:

> Business interests urge an aggressive national policy and businessmen direct it. Such a policy is warlike as well as patriotic. The direct cultural value of a warlike business policy is unequivocal. It makes for a conservative animus on the part of the populace. During war time, and within the military organization at all times, under martial law, civil rights are in abeyance; and the more warfare and armament the more abeyance. . . . A military organization is a servile organization. Insubordination is the deadly sin (II, 391).

What is true of those directly involved in the military applies also to the civilian population in significant degree:

> They learn to think in warlike terms of rank, authority, and subordination, and so grow progressively more patient of encroachments upon their civil rights . . . (II, 392). At the same stroke they [patriotic ideals] direct the popular interest to other, nobler, institutionally less hazardous matters than the unequal distribution of wealth or of creature comforts (II, 393).

But for those who might see this as a triumph of business enterprise over the threat of social change led by workers, it is turned by Veblen into a hollow triumph. For, if the discipline and values of the warlike and patriotic society may "correct" the institutionally disintegrative trend of the machine process, it is just as probable that, for the same reasons, there would be "a rehabilitation of the ancient patriotic animosity and dynastic loyalty, to the relative neglect of business interests. This may easily be carried so far as to sacrifice the profits of the businessman to the exigencies of the higher politics" (II, 395).

Thus, Veblen sees the system of business enterprise caught in a terrible historical dilemma: If, to offset the institutional and threatening imperatives of industrialism, it encourages, or acquiesces in, developments that will cause social unrest to "sink in the broad sands of patriotism," it is faced with the equal probability that what is quicksand for one will sooner or later pull down the other.

The last paragraph of the *Theory* might be Veblen's epitaph for the system of business enterprise:

It seems possible to say this much, that the full dominion of business enterprise is necessarily a transitory dominion. It stands to lose in the end whether the one or the other of the two divergent cultural tendencies wins, because it is incompatible with the ascendancy of either (II, 400).*

---

* Thus, in the late 1930's, German industrialists who had supported Nazism as a "corrective discipline" for the p͟   ͟al and economic troubles of the early 1930's found themselves increasi͟ngly harassed by regulation, taxation, and general interference in their affairs by Nazi Party and Wehrmacht functionaries.

Chapter 3

VEBLEN AND ECONOMIC THEORY

Say "Veblen" to a passing economist, and he will most likely think "institutionalism," and then "anti-theory." eblen is credited (or debited) with being the progenitor of institutional economics—a grab bag whose contents include everything from finely machined analytical instruments and hypotheses to patches of crazy quilt. Despite having been labeled as anti-theory, many, perhaps most, institutional economists consider themselves to be theorists.

Veblen's writings were almost always occupied with theorizing and theory, and he was scornful of mere cataloguers and describers—what he called "taxonomists." But it is this very characteristic for which Veblen and the institutionalists are themselves scorned by the economic "theorists" today. What is the explanation for this thoroughgoing confusion?

The answer has more than one side to it. Some of the severest critics of Veblen and other institutionalists are only barely acquainted with their extensive theoretical writings; much has been written by self-styled followers of Veblen, or those to whom Veblenism is attributed, where neither their ideas nor Veblen's provide much support for the connection. (Most notorious of these, perhaps, were the "Technocrats" of the 1930's.)

More basic than the foregoing, however, is the perennial controversy over "theory" in the field of economics: What is, or should be, the aim of theory? What procedures or methods are acceptable and desirable? When is a theory "good" or "bad"? In short, what is the appropriate scope and method of economics? Those who denigrate Veblen as being un- or anti-theoretical, if they are saying anything that can be supported, are differing with his *version* of theory—no less, it may be added, than he did (or would) with theirs.*

As earlier chapters have suggested, Veblen theorized much about his world. But he also theorized about theory itself; i.e., he concerned himself with *methodology,* as is frequently true and necessary for innovators. Veblen's most important writings in this area have been collected in *The Place of Science in Modern Civilization.* In these (and other) essays, Veblen 1) analyzed the general factors affecting and shaping the development of science in general and economic science in particular; 2) analyzed why and in what sense economics, in his view, had strayed from promising paths of inquiry and method, and made clear what he took the latter to be; 3) criticized the dominant economic theory of his day ("marginal-utility economics"), and 4) on the same bases and with much the same reasoning, criticized Marxian economic theory. Although Veblen's methodological essays are largely critical, elements of his own views emerge as his analysis develops.**

A fundamental assumption for Veblen is the tentative and relativistic quality of both the procedures and the findings of science. The basis for his viewpoint is twofold: 1) the evolutionary, or constantly changing, nature of social existen and 2) the (changing) impact which society has on the preconceptions, or largely unconscious assumptions, of its members—including its scientists.

---

* "Theory," as it will be discussed below, is what today is classified as "*micro*-theory," the theory of the firm, of demand, of partial equilibrium, and the like. "*Macro*-theory," which analyzes the behavior of the economy as a whole—e.g., its expansion and contraction —did not become a leading subject of economics until the 1930's. Up to that time, with unimportant and technical exceptions, conventional economists had assumed away the issues dealt with in "macrotheory." Veblen's own theorizing did not break economic analysis into such compartments; as we saw, in our discussion of *The Theory of Business Enterprise,* his discussion of business behavior on the level of the enterprise is integrated with his discussion of, e.g., depression.

** The following critical examination of neo-classical economics (what Veblen called "marginal-utility economics") is presented as Veblen saw it; in Chapter 5 the examination of this and Veblen's own economics will be approached from a contemporary position.

As a general approach, this was neither unique nor original. Its scientific foundation for Veblen was the evolutionary theory of Darwin, to which Veblen explicitly and frequently acknowledged indebtedness. The relativistic viewpoint was put forth long before Veblen; one can find its seeds in Heraclitus, centuries before Christ. In nineteenth century social theory, however, the most insistent proponent of this view was Karl Marx, who expressed the notion succinctly when he said, "It is not the consciousness of men that determines their existence, but, on the contrary, their social existence determines their consciousness."*

If one views science as affecting and affected by the evolutionary social process, it follows that both the scientist's focus and his theoretical conclusions are and must be ephemeral. This is so not merely because we are enabled to understand *more* over time, as improving technology and accumulating knowledge help clear the woods for the scientist; it is also because we are socially stimulated and able to understand more, and in different terms—in answer to different questions, and with different implications. The growth of scientific understanding is not simply cumulative, in this view, it is also, in good part, as it has often been said, "the process of disproving hypotheses."

Veblen did not posit that the *data* analyzed by the biological and physical scientists change; these could be taken as given, for analytical purposes. What he saw as changing is the world-view, the preconceptions, the matters taken for granted or questioned by the probing scientist. Thus, we have a Newton in one era, and an Einstein in another—both scientific geniuses, both honest and meticulous in their procedures, but, although seemingly treating the "same data," coming to quite different theoretical conclusions.

For the social scientist, the situation is much more complicated. Not only do societies evolve more quickly than,

---

* In the Preface of *The Critique of Political Economy.* But Veblen and Marx differed in the manner in which they held this view, as well as about the shape and determinants of the process of social change—Veblen following Darwin, and Marx adapting the Hegelian schema.

say, the flora and fauna; the analyst is himself part of, and shaped by, the data he is analyzing. Although he can be *objective,* he cannot be *neutral.* Objectivity is observed when scientific procedures are followed; but neutrality, i.e., indifference to results, is neither possible nor desirable.

Veblen insisted upon something else: Not only is the social scientist involved in the results he develops, his involvement is critically defined by the *questions* he asks. The questions asked are in turn defined by the problems deemed important by the analyst; and what is deemed a problem is a product of the viewer's social values, as affected by his time, place, and background. Thus, the point of view of the economists "has always been in large part the point of view of the enlightened common sense of their time. The spiritual attitude of a given generation of economists is therefore in good part a special outgrowth of the ideals and preconceptions current in the world about them" (VIII, 86). These "ideals and preconceptions" lead men to appraise a given situation as "normal" or "abnormal," or as holding forth promise or threat.

Of the many factors shaping the social scientist's outlook, one is the general state of scientific thinking itself. Veblen was profoundly convinced that fruitful and scientific social analysis must utilize and accord with the evolutionary viewpoint—more exactly, that social analysis must be *genetic,* an analysis of process. This viewpoint led Veblen to emphasize *institutions* as the central focus of social analysis.

Unlike many social scientists of his own time—and perhaps some still today—Veblen took seriously the view of man as an animal, whose career and behavior must be analyzed in terms of biological evolution, albeit with appropriate modifications for the characteristics peculiar to our species—particularly the capacity "to take thought." "Men take thought," he wrote, "but the human spirit, that is to say the racial endowment of instinctive proclivities, decides what they shall take thought of, and how and to what effect" (III, 6).

According to Veblen, the "lower animals," when compared to man, are relatively passive with respect to their environment, and the process of physical evolution (for man and other animals) is relatively much slower than that of the social evolution which so sharply affects man's life and livelihood; but man is still a species of animal subject to the laws of evolution, both in his physical and his social characteristics. The senses in which man must be contrasted with, say, bears, lead us to focus on the development of, and the relationships between, technology and social institutions—where both are the outcome of man's capacity to think, and to pass on to his descendants accumulated knowledge and technique. "The higher the degree of intelligence and the larger the available body of knowledge current in any given community, the more extensive and elaborate will be the logic of the ways and means interposed between these impulses and their realization, and the more multifarious and complicated will be the apparatus of expedients and resources employed to compass those ends that are instinctively worth while" (III, 6).

Man is a *social* creature—one whose aspirations, abilities, needs, and achievements are a product of social activity. If the behavior and the problems of man are to be understood, declares Veblen, the point of departure for analysis must be that of man developing in society i.e., the social institutions devised by man that guide his behavior. For Veblen the social sciences must focus upon institutions; they must study process and relationship, must make a genetic inquiry into institutions, addressing itself "to the growth of habits and conventions, as conditioned by the material environment and by the innate and persistent propensities of human nature . . ." (III, 2).

The leading question for Veblen was "What's next, and why?" To answer that question, one must know what has *preceded* and what *is*—i.e., scientific inquiry into social questions must be characterized by empirical inquiries of past and present. But such inquiry constitutes a mere beginning. There must be a theoretical framework to guide the investigator through the morass of infinite "facts." Without a set of selective principles, inquiry must be endless and futile—and merely descriptive.

Theorizing implies abstracting from certain aspects of

complex reality, in order to focus upon, and be able to analyze, essentials. Where Veblen differed from conventional economic theorists was not in his use or eschewal of abstraction, but in his definition of "essentials."* What conventional economists in Veblen's time (and subsequently) examined and what they took as given will be discussed in detail later; suffice to point out here that they abstracted from the very matters Veblen saw as most requiring attention: technological change, the nature and function of economic and legal institutions, and the process of social change resulting from the interaction of these.

Like the neo-classicists, Veblen took technological change as "given"; unlike them, Veblen integrated the *consequences* of technological change into his analysis. The neo-classicists paid little attention to the institutional meaning of technology at any point in time, and completely ignored its consequences over time, attempting rather to elucidate what would happen in the *absence* of change. In the lengthy quotation that follows, the objects of Veblen's criticism are the economists of his day, whom he is taking to task for neglecting what he takes to be essential.

There are certain saving clauses in common use . . . : "Given the state of the industrial arts"; "Other things remaining the same"; "In the long run"; "In the absence of disturbing causes." It has been the praiseworthy endeavor of the votaries of this established law and custom to hold fast the good old plan on a strategic line of interpretation resting on these provisos. There have been painstaking elucidations of what is fundamental and intrinsic in the way of human institutions, of what essentially ought to be, and of what must eventually come to pass in the natural course of time and change as it is believed to run along under the guidance of those

---

* This difference, however, which led Veblen to concentrate heavily on institutions, meant that he could not operate on as rarefied a level of abstraction as those he criticized. The level of generality in the hands of many economic theorists has become so elevated as to suggest that abstraction has become an end in itself.

indefeasible principles that make up the modern point of view. And the disquieting incursions of the New Order have been disallowed as not being of the essence of Nature's contract with mankind, within the constituent principles of the modern point of view stabilized in the eighteenth century.

Now. . . , the state of the industrial arts has at no time continued unchanged during the modern era; consequently other things have never remained the same; and in the long run the outcome has always been shaped by the disturbing causes. All this reflects no discredit on the economists and publicists who have sketched out the natural run of the present and future in the dry light of the eighteenth-century principles, since their reservations have not been observed. The arguments have been as good as the premises on which they proceed, and the premises have once been good enough to command unquestioning assent; although that is now some time ago. The fault appears to lie in the unexampled shifty behavior of the latterday facts (VII, 85-86).

Although Veblen criticized his colleagues for their procedures, he dissented even more fundamentally from their questions. In effect, these amounted to: "Given that what exists is natural and largely desirable, how preserve and refine it?" For Veblen this was an unscientific question, and an instance of means having become ends in a complicated socio-psychological process.

Under the discipline of habituation the logic and apparatus of ways and means falls into conventional lines, acquires the consistency of custom and prescription, and so takes on an institutional character and force. The accustomed ways of doing and thinking not only become an habitual matter of course, easy and obvious, but they come likewise to be sanctioned by social convention, and so become right and proper and give rise to principles of conduct. By use and wont they are incorporated into the current scheme of common sense. As elements of the approved scheme of conduct and pursuit these conventional ways and means take their place as proximate ends of endeavor. Whence, in the further course of unremitting habituation, as the attention is habitually focussed on these proximate ends, . . . their own ulterior purpose [is] often . . . lost sight of . . . (III, 7, 8).

If all this seems obvious to the reader, its implications for the economists of Veblen's day, and later, were less so. At this point it will be appropriate to examine the economic theory against which Veblen was reacting. Having done that, we may go on to see what changes have taken place since Veblen wrote. (In our concluding chapter, we shall examine what, from a Veblenian standpoint, remains to be done.)

Writing in 1898, Veblen felt moved t observe that ". . . economics is helplessly behind the times, and unable to handle its subject-matter in a way to entitle it to standing as a modern science. . . . Nor are the economists themselves buoyantly indifferent to the rebuke. . . . With the economists who are most attentively looked to for guidance, uncertainty as to the definitive value of what has been and is being done, and as to what we may, with effect, take to next, is so common as to suggest that indecision is a meritorious work" (VIII, 56-57.) *

The focus of Veblen's critical essays in economic theory was largely "neo-classical economics," always referred to by Veblen as "marginal-utility economics." This stage in the development of economic thought was beginning to claim at-

---

* That changes since 1898 leave much yet to be done in the discipline before it can claim scientific status may be gathered by the largely negative views expressed at the 1962 Meetings of the American Economic Association. Harvard's E. S. Mason, in his presidential address, after castigating the profession for "sheer ignorance," and a continuing inability to know "what's next," complained that "the economist tends to ignore or underrate the importance of institutions —of the real-world individuals and groups in business, labor, and government. . . ." For this and other leading economists' similarly dour views, see *Business Week*, January 5, 1963, pp. 18-19.

tention in Veblen's youth, had become dominant as he matured, and remained dominant up to his death in 1929. In the years since 1929—years of depression, world war, and pervasive interest in economic development—economics has changed in important ways, some of them away from, and some elaborating, the neo-classical format. But the approach of neo-classicism dies hard—if at all—as indicated by its continuing central role in economics textbooks. Veblen's analysis of the economics of his day still has pertinence, therefore; assuming that his criticisms were valid, it becomes worthwhile to set forth their principal features.

Veblen's critique was based upon what the marginalists assumed, or assumed away, concerning man, economic behavior, and society, and what they ignored in the matters under analysis. In effect, Veblen attacked the questions asked, the manner in which the answers were gained, and the answers themselves.

If for Veblen the question was "what's next, and why?" the question for the neo-classical economist, as another critic has put it, was "why and when does an egg cost more than a cup of tea?" For the neo-classical economists the central problem of economics revolved around the allocation of scarce resources among competing uses—and this led them to construct their theories in terms of relative pricing, valuation, and distribution. The materials from which their analytical tools were formed were inherited from the utilitarians: the hedonistic psychological stuff of anticipated pleasure and pain.*

Apart from the fact that the hedonistic psychology had been pushed aside by Veblen's day—by psychologists, not by economists—it was his point that such an approach was in any event largely off the mark, and unscientific to boot. Even if the hedonistic calculus were valid, it would explain only a part, and an unimportant part, of the economic prob-

---

* Among the leading neo-classicists were Léon Walras, Carl Menger, W. S. Jevons, and (most influential, best informed, most restrained of all) Alfred Marshall. One of Veblen's most frequent targets was an early mentor, John Bates Clark, father of one of Veblen's most distinguished followers, John Maurice Clark.

lems analyzed. And if this were not enough, for Veblen the problem itself was relatively unimportant.

For Veblen, scientific social analysis meant a cause and effect analysis, an analysis of process and relationship. The marginalist analysis was based upon "sufficient reason" rather than "efficient cause"—it was teleological. By this term, which recurs frequently in his critique, Veblen meant that explanation of an event was cast in terms of what was (presumably) to follow the event rather than what preceded it. In the neo-classical framework,

> . . . human conduct is conceived of and interpreted as a rational response to the exigencies of the situation in which mankind is placed; as regards economic conduct it is such a rational and unprejudiced response to the stimulus of anticipated pleasure and pain—being, typically and in the main, a response to the promptings of anticipated pleasure, for the hedonists of the nineteenth century and of the marginal-utility school are in the main of an optimistic temper. . . . Men's activities differ, therefore, (inconsiderably) in respect of the alertness of the response and nicety of adjustment of irksome pain-cost to apprehended future sensuous gain; but, on the whole no other ground or line or guidance of conduct than this rationalistic calculus falls properly within the cognizance of the economic hedonists. Such a theory can take account of conduct only in so far as it is rational conduct, guided by deliberate and exhaustively intelligent choice—wise adaptation to the demands of the main chance (VIII, 234-35).

Veblen took account of man's rationality, his looking ahead, in his view of man as "taking thought"; and took this aspect of man as necessarily a *part* of any scientific analysis of his behavior. But the greater influence on man is that of habituation, convention, and circumstance. Veblen did not criticize conventional economics for including the rational element of man's nature in its analysis, but rather because "by force of its postulates its attention is *confined* to this teleological bearing of conduct alone" (VIII, 239. My emphasis.). To broaden the analytical framework to allow in the influence of institutions (habituation, convention, and circumstance) would be to examine the very matters that the marginal-utility economists took for granted; namely, the "principles of action which underlie the current, business-like scheme of economic life. . . , not to be called into question without questioning the existing law and order" (VIII, 239).

Neo-classical economists were optimistic. Their view of man as a rational creature was itself a variant of optimism, and they were explicitly optimistic about the future of mankind. In this they were at one with Karl Marx and with the Victorian age in which their ideas were developed; it was an age of worldwide economic expansion and, for many in the industrializing countries, one in which horizons were limitless. Their optimism may be understood as an easy by-product of buoyancy and expansion. What is less easy to understand is the assumption that their economic world was for analytical purposes foursquare with that of Adam Smith.* Not only the economic world—i.e., of small-scale technology and enterprise—but its philosophical assumptions of a beneficent, natural and normal, order are implicit in neo-classical analysis. Thus, the neo-classical theory considers the "representative firm," in which decisions are made by a rational entrepreneur, operating within a market about which he has adequate knowledge and over which he has no control, where advertising and sales promotion are neither necessary nor likely, where the labor force and its productivity are known and knowable, capital is scarce, markets are buoyant (there is no involuntary unemployment), and the consequences of decisions are predictable and fully taken into account.

* Even more intriguing is the widespread inclination of contemporary economists to work with a theory assuming the economic world of Smith and based on the optimism of the past century. This is not to say that economists are unaware of the technology and institutions of their world, nor that they are themselves optimistic. But that is what underlies the core of "theory" still today.

To all this we may contrast Veblen's view of man, of business, and of technology. For all practical and theoretical purposes, Veblen and the neo-classical economists were talking about different worlds. Veblen argued that their world was a compound of the dead past and unrestrained imagination and he gave a sardonic interpretation of the neo-classicist's "economic man," an interpretation that has become classic:

The hedonistic conception of man is that of a lightning calculator of pleasures and pains, who oscillates like a homogeneous globule of desire of happiness under the impulse of stimuli that shift him about the area, but leave him intact. He has neither antecedent nor consequent. He is an isolated, definitive human datum, in stable equilibrium except for the buffets of the impinging forces that displace him in one direction or another. Self-imposed in elemental space, he spins symmetrically about his own spiritual axis until the parallelogram of forces bears down upon him, whereupon he follows the line of the resultant. When the force of the impact is spent, he comes to rest, a self-contained globule of desire as before (VIII, 73-74).

This economic man plays several roles. As a consumer, he balances marginal utilities off against each other. As a worker, he calculates the pain-cost of an additional unit of work, and compares that pain against the satisfaction he expects to gain from spending his wages. As an entrepreneur, economic man is involved in the most elaborate calculations and estimates: his own anticipated pleasure (derived from his profits and their use); the calculations of those who buy from him; and his own pain-cost (caused by his expenditures on capital, labor and materials, and his own efforts).

Even if the marginal-utility economics were concerned with realistic essentials, the theory, expressed as it is in terms of psychological sensations of pain and pleasure, would be unworkable for practical purposes and unverifiable. The economic world is one in which magnitudes are those of weight and measure, dollars and cents, prices and quantities.*

Behavior in the market is understood in terms of the "representative firm," which, manned by rational entrepreneurs, will respond to stimuli in the following fashion: through the inexorable workings of the law of supply and demand, and assuming no change in institutions, no involuntary unemployment, no significant change in technology, a "normal equilibrium" will result. Resources will then be so allocated that society receives the maximum satisfaction from its limited resources. In addition, workers, owners, and entrepreneurs will be rewarded exactly in proportion as they have contributed to production, and the role of the state—assumed to be minimal, as a genial and aloof night watchman —will (and should) be kept to the irreducible minimum.

All this ignores the preponderant influence of large-scale productive techniques in the economy, and the relationship of this to the size, nature, aims, and pressures of the large corporation endowed with decision-making powers. According to Veblen,

The time, place, rate and material conditions of the work in hand are determined immediately by the mechanically standardized process in which the given plant is engaged; and beyond that all these matters are dependent on the exigencies and manoeuvres of business, largely by way of moderating the rate of production and keeping the output reasonably short of maximum capacity. The workman has become subsidiary to the mechanical equipment, and productive industry has become subservient to business, in all those countries which have come in for the latterday state of the industrial arts, and which so have fallen under the domination of the price system (VII, 38-39).

---

*In the hands of Marshall, particularly, although the focus was on the "representative firm" operating in the unreal world of the neo-classicists, the behavior of buyers and sellers had become a function of *price*. But this was merely a formal change. Underlying both demand and supply, and determining them, remained the hedonistic calculus.

Veblen's further objection to the method of neo-classical economics was its conscious or unconscious adherence to the concepts of natural law, as refined in the eighteenth century. The idea of a "natural" or "normal" state of "equilibrium" (to which matters do or should tend) stood in contrast to what Veblen saw as the blind drift of evolution, determined by "opaque cause and effect." Veblen thought that man was able to affect his destiny; but he also thought that the manner in which man could do so was determined by the context (historical and present) in which he found himself. His background, his situation, and his needs define his possibilities, and they offer relatively narrow limits within which rational choice may or will be exercised.

As for the "representative firm," and the "normal" economic situation, Veblen, in one of his sourer moods, chose to characterize these as

> . . . business as usual; which means working at cross-purposes as usual, waste of work and materials as usual, restriction of output as usual, unemployment as usual, labor quarrels as usual, competitive selling as usual, mendacious advertising as usual, waste of superfluities as usual by the kept classes, and privation as usual for the common man (VII, 141).

And he adds: "All of which may conceivably be put up with by this people 'lest a worse evil befall' " (*Ibid.*).

From his very first essay, Veblen's economic theory was concerned with an economy plagued by combinations in restraint of trade, unemployment and excess capacity, and irrational waste of effort and resources. If most of his fellow theorists were able to posit a harmonious world of rationality and efficiency, and go on to deduce appropriate theorems, their ability to do so was rudely assaulted by the events which ensued after 1929, the year of Veblen's death. In that year, the world careened into a disastrous depression, and proceeded to exhibit itself in a fashion that might have surprised even Veblen.

In the United States, industrial production fell by about

half between 1929 and 1933; conservatively measured, unemployment rose to a quarter of the labor force. It no longer took a jaundiced, or even a careful, eye to see that economic behavior was determined by something less than a subjective rationality and that such a determination left much to be desired.

This is not the place to detail either the causes or the manifestations of the depression of the thirties; nor can we examine here the many and resulting permutations of economic analysis developed during and since that period. Suffice it to say that the economy after 1929 faced 1) drastically reduced production, employment, and income, and only moderately falling prices (particularly in industry); 2) revelations of an extraordinary range of malfeasance amounting almost to depravity in the world of finance; and 3) devastating numbers of bankruptcies throughout the economy. Associated with the foregoing were 4) millions of unemployed desperately and futilely seeking jobs, 5) significant and substantially successful movements to organize industrial workers, and 6) a world economy undergoing a shattering contraction in the volume of trade and an equally shattering proliferation of the weapons and attitudes of economic nationalism. Among the political consequences were 7) the persistent demand by farmers that they be released from the thralldom of the free market, and 8) a greatly expanded rôle for government in the economy. In the face of all this, and more, economists could scarcely continue to theorize in terms of questions that, if anything, shed light on the relative prices of "an egg and a cup of tea," working within a framework of assumptions daily shouted down in the headlines.

Economics did not suddenly, completely, or adequately transform itself in the midst of this chaos—the dead hand of the past is not light—but most economists did begin to pay closer attention to the real world, with rewarding results in analysis and in research. Theories that did much—if not enough—to explain alternating periods of economic expansion and contraction, and persistent unemployment, were constructed (mixing Keynes with much of what Wesley Clair Mitchell, a follower of Veblen, had developed before the crisis). The concepts and tools of social accounting were devised to relate theory to reality; the neo-classical format of perfectly competitive (and, almost as an afterthought, purely monopolistic) markets was joined to (highly abstract) theories of imperfect and monopolistic competition. These in turn stimulated industry studies of real-life business situations and attempts to develop a theory of concentrated ("oligopolistic") markets about which Veblen had theorized in 1904—markets in which a few sellers dominate and act together to achieve their separate ends. A whole school of labor economists, owing much to the earlier work of John R. Commons, an "institutionalist," and bent on understanding the workings of labor markets, came into existence. Still more recently, economists, reacting to the problems of growth in the industrialized countries and to the desperate attempts of the "underdeveloped" to industrialize, have turned in increasing numbers to an examination of the factors holding back and contributing to change and development. In all these shifts in the economists' focus, and most especially in the last-named, economists have rediscovered the need to understand *institutions*.

Economics had begun that way, in the hands of Adam Smith. Whether or not economics will continue to move along promising paths of inquiry, and move along ther with theoretical constructs well designed for the task in hand, is not yet clear. Today the methods, techniques, and theoretical apparatus by which economists theorize are determined to a surprising degree by what their teachers train them to do* in the economics departments of leading universities. There the characteristics mocked by Veblen—prestige, tradition, a distaste for novelty and for imprecision, a confusion between "objectivity" and "neutrality," a certain affinity for what is, and a host of psychological factors beyond the ken of an economist—contribute to a continuing en-

---

* Smith was a professor of Moral Philosophy. It is an open question whether or not he would today gain the ear of the economics profession (making the appropriate changes for time, place, and arguments), or even a Ph.D.

shrinement of the neo-classical format, with all else relegated to the status of an unkempt (if large and demanding) stepchild.

One symptom of this continuing malaise has been the close to spectacular emergence of two fields within economics—mathematical economics and econometrics. Practitioners of the former concern themselves mostly, but not entirely, with the neo-classical "variables," questions, and assumptions, and their achievement frequently consists of thrusting into outer space what had earlier rested untroubled in the stratosphere. The econometricians—for all practical purposes, economists using highly refined statistical techniques—can and often do concern themselves with data drawn from reality, rather than from assumption. But they, like their mathematical kin, most frequently find pleasure and prestige in manipulating data that will yield "elegant" results. The generalization may be made—to which there are honorable exceptions—that the elegance moves in direct proportion with irrelevance to economic problems.

A significant and growing number of "old-fashioned" economists view the rapid expansion of these two sub-disciplines with qualified approval, if with increasing mystification. Such economists point out—and with reason—that the new techniques can be, and sometimes are, used to grapple with important problems; that abstraction and quantification are of course necessary ingredients of meaningful economic theory.[*]

The question is not *whether* such techniques can be useful, but in whose hands they can be, and how many hands can sensibly be used in this way—considering the range of important economic problems that *cannot* be understood with such techniques. It is a question of allocating scarce resources to competing ends.

The problem here is relatively subtle. Students with mathematical prowess are increasingly drawn into economics

---

[*] With which Veblen agreed. Ironically, some of Veblen's followers are most gripped by the notion that *only* that which is quantifiable is in the true domain of economics—with which Veblen disagreed, as exemplified in his own work.

by this development, not because of their interest in economic problems but because of their facility in mathematics. Such interests lead these students to slight the "institutional" aspects of economics, with the consequence that their own contributions (in teaching and in writing) are likely to be constructed less in terms of realistic assumptions and urgent issues than in terms of what is most susceptible of graceful formulae and computer manipulation. In the hands of a well-trained, "old-fashioned" economist, this danger is minimized, although it is not eliminated. The danger does not inhere in the techniques, but in those who, if only out of ignorance —Veblen would call it "trained incapacity"—misuse techniques. The attitudes and institutions of the system of higher learning in America do little to assuage such fears.*

All these efforts may one day produce work which, though seemingly unrelated to reality, will, like the basic research of the natural sciences, break paths for those working closer to the forest. The activities of the more elegant economists would be merely interesting, were it not that their influence within the profession is already large and growing apace. To critics of this latest development, it is a melancholy instance of Gresham's Law: bad money drives out good.

In writing of Veblen's analysis of economic theory and of economists, one can say that, given Veblen's sociological and relativistic analysis of the development of science, the current developments—both toward and away from his own position—would not have surprised him. The dramatic and urgent economic problems of the world have impelled many to stare the untidy facts in the face, if with discomfort; the presently substantial rewards for *not* doing so have allowed others to turn their backs upon these facts. A prophecy as to the outcome is impossible.

So much for Veblen and conventional economic theory. In his day, rumbling underground, was a fully developed and increasingly influential system of distinctly unconven-

---

* See the Appendix on *The Higher Learning in America* for Veblen's analysis of this matter. The general problem just discussed is taken up in a related manner in our concluding chapter.

tional economics: Marxian economic theory. In temperament, method, and conclusions, Veblen was much closer to Marx than to the neo-classicists. But he was also quite different in all these respects.

Marxian economic theory is an immensely complicated body of thought, combining history, philosophy, economics, and sociology. As Veblen warned,

> Except as a whole and except in the light of its postulates and aims, the Marxian system is not only not tenable, but it is not even intelligible. A discussion of a given isolated feature of the system (such as the theory of value) . . . is as futile as a discussion of solids in terms of two dimensions (VIII, 410).

In his analysis of Marxian theory, Veblen paid most attention to 1) the "dialectical" process of change, 2) the principal forces or agents making for change and their relationship to the economic characteristics (or tendencies) of capitalist development, and 3) the presumed outcome of all these taken together: namely, socialism.

Characteristically, Veblen's critique takes Marx on his own terms and in his own time. If Veblen was critical of Marx, he was also largely contemptuous of those other critics whose analyses were colored by similar or deeper defects. Veblen had a high regard for Marx as a profound and prodigious thinker, and as an imposing propagandist:

> As to the motives which drive him and the aspirations which guide him, in destructive criticism and in creative speculation alike, he is primarily a theoretician busied with the analysis of economic phenomena and their organization into a consistent and faithful system of scientific knowledge; but he is, at the same time, consistently and tenaciously alert to the bearing which each step in the progress of his theoretical work has upon the propaganda. His work has, therefore, an air of bias, such as belongs to an advocate's argument; but it is not, therefore, to be assumed, nor indeed to be credited, that his

propagandist aims have in any substantial way deflected his inquiry of his speculations from the faithful pursuit of scientific truth. His socialistic bias may color his polemics, but his logical grasp is too neat and firm to admit of any bias, other than that of his metaphysical preconceptions, affecting his theoretical work (VIII, 410).

But when Veblen points to "metaphysical preconceptions," he is opening a yawning pit; in the case of Marx, it is a pit that in Veblen's hands becomes a grave. The principal repository of Marx's metaphysical preconceptions, as Veblen saw matters, was his "materialistic conception of history." That conception is one of

movement, development, evolution, progress; and . . . the movement is conceived necessarily to take place by the method of conflict or struggle. The movement is of the nature of progress,—gradual advance toward a goal, toward the realization in explicit form of all that is implicit in the substantial activity involved in the movement. The movement is, further, self-conditioned and self-acting: it is an unfolding by inner necessity. The struggle which constitutes the method of movement or evolution is, in the Hegelian system proper [which Marxian theory derived from, but transformed], the struggle of the spirit for self-realisation by the process of the well-known three-phase dialectic [: thesis, antithesis, synthesis]. In the materialistic conception of history this dialectical movement becomes the class struggle of the Marxian system (VIII, 414-15).

Like Marx, Veblen saw change as continuous, and as taking place as a result of conflict—adaptation to and resolution of the unremitting interaction between technological change and outmoded institutions. It was not Marx's notion of continuous change nor his preoccupation with conflict that jarred Veblen. It was Marx's assumption of particular kinds of conflict, having a particular basis, and a particular outcome, that Veblen deemed metaphysical and therefore unscientific.

For Veblen the dialectical course of change—involving the interpenetration of opposites, contradictions, and syntheses—was inadequate either as a figure of speech or as a basis for prediction. Like the philosophical framework of the neo-classical economists, it was teleological. It was also based on overly optimistic assumptions concerning man and his future.

The concrete social phenomenon Marx saw as the prime agency of change was the class struggle, conceived of as having a "materialistic" base. But, said Veblen,

the term "material" is in this connection used in a meta-phorical sense. It does not mean mechanical or physical, or even physiological, but economic. It is material in the sense that it is a struggle between classes for the ma-terial means of life. . . . The dialectic of the movement of social progress, therefore, moves on the spiritual plane of human desire and passion, not on the (literally) material plane of mechanical and physiological stress, on which the developmental process of brute creation unfolds itself (VIII, 415).

Like the neo-classicists, according to Veblen, Marx as-sumed rational behavior on the part of man—both business-man and workingman. Veblen was fully cognizant of the rational quality of man, but he considered it but one aspect of the matters determining his behavior. The class struggle as Marx developed it was a conscious one, assuming re-flection and a knowledge of relevant fact. In addition, Marx assumed that other factors playing on man—we may call them "irrational," meaning non-economic—are subordinated or ineffectual. According to Veblen, looked at in Darwinian terms and drained of nineteenth-century optimism, the Marxian process of social change is distorted in some degree in every feature, and "a shadow of doubt" falls on every conclusion. In Marxian theory, according to Veblen, the exigencies of the material means of life control the conduct of men in society throughout, and thereby indefeasibly guide the growth of institutions and shape every shifting trait of human culture. . . . , through men's taking thought of material (economic) advantages and disadvantages, and choosing that which will yield the fuller material measure of life. When the materialistic conception passes under the Darwinian norm, of cumulative causation, it happens, first, that this initial principle itself is reduced to the rank of a habit of thought induced in the speculator who depends on its light, by the circumstances of his life, in the way of hereditary bent, occupation, tradition, education, climate, food supply, and the like. But. . . , whether and how far [the] traits of human culture and the institutional structure built ᴏut of them are the outgrowth of material (economic) exigencies becomes a question of what kind and degree of efficiency belongs to the economic exigencies among the complex of circumstances that conduce to the formation of habits. It is no longer a question of whether material exigencies rationally should guide men's conduct, but whether, as a matter of brute causation, they do . . . (VIII, 437-38).

Veblen, unlike most critics of Marx, did not have an aversion to socialism. Neither did he view society as an harmonious mechanism or organism; he saw conflict as perpetual and as the "natural" state of affairs. What Veblen did object to was the teleological notion that because of social conflict society was moving toward a *particular* and *desirable* resolution, guided by conscious and rational effort. As a Darwinian, he could not accept a conscious class struggle "as the one necessary method of social progress" (VIII, 416).

For Veblen the process of social change was not determined by the conflict between the desirable and the undesirable, with an ultimate resolution in favor of the former. Society is a bubbling cauldron, to be sure; but more than the popping bubbles must be taken into account. What underlies

the bubbles is the dense weight of the past, of tradition, of habituation, and the ongoing propensities of man.

Veblen did not doubt for a moment that the "vested interests" (loosely, Marx's "capitalists") were determined to hold what they had and to use their power to that end. As in Marx, technological change in the Veblenian scheme was a constant, and a continuing and enlarging irritant in the oyster of social stability. Again, as for Marx, the "underlying population" (Marx's "proletariat"), particularly the industrial working class, finds abundant reason for discontent with its lot in society. But, because the reasons for this last are different in Veblen than in Marx, the predicted result is also different.

Marx was well aware of the enormous productive achievements of industrial capitalism, and of its even greater potential, as early as 1848, the year of *The Communist Manifesto*. But this was not his emphasis. Among Marx's many predictions concerning the course of capitalist development were 1) the increasing misery of the working class, and 2) the polarization of society into powerful capitalists and proletarians—i.e., the elimination of the petty middle class (and the small farmer). At the time he wrote, these were reasonable (if not entirely accurate) inferences for Marx to draw from the life around him. This was mostly *British* life in the middle of the nineteenth century, unsettled by rapid industrial development, great structural change in the economy, Chartist and other movements of agitation, and, by and large, showing abundant evidences to support Marx's theories—including an unusually prominent place for economic criteria in the conduct of all social affairs. Veblen was to comment on these same problems half a century later. What he saw then led to a powerful demurrer, both as regarded the facts and the theory:

. . . the result of the last few decades of our industrial development has been to increase greatly the creature comforts within the reach of the average human being. And, decidedly, the result has been an amelioration of the lot of the less favored in a relatively greater degree than that of those economically more fortunate. The claim that the system of competition has proved itself an engine for making the rich richer and the poor poorer has the fascination of an epigram; but if its meaning is that the lot of the average, of the masses of humanity in civilized life, is worse today as measured in the means of livelihood, than it was twenty, or fifty, or a hundred years ago, then it is farcical (VIII, 391).

But suppose that steady "immiserization" was the fact of industrial capitalist development?* Would such a development promote "a well-advised and well-consolidated working-class movement"? Far from it:

. . . so soon as the question is approached on Darwinian ground of cause and effect, and is analyzed in terms of habit and of response to stimulus, the doctrine that progressive misery must effect a socialistic revolution becomes dubious, and very shortly untenable. Experience, the experience of history, teaches that abject misery carries with it deterioration and abject subjection (VIII, 443).

Still, there was discontent. What was its source? Here we are drawn back to one of Veblen's fundamental concepts, emulation, as developed most fully in his *Theory of the Leisure Class*. It is not the abjectly miserable who possess the ability or the inclination to spearhead the forces of discontent (nor did they do so in Marx—who termed them "lumpenproletariat."). It is those who are strong enough to improve themselves, and their attempt will not be to stay alive, but "to keep up appearances." What Veblen has to say on this score does much to explain twentieth-century patterns of work and consumption.

The existing system has not made, and does not tend to make, the industrious poor poorer as measured ab-

* In this context, Veblen was referring only to developments within the industrial societies.

solutely in means of livelihood; but it does tend to make them relatively poorer, in their own eyes, as measured in terms of comparative economic importance, and, curious as it may seem at first sight, that is what seems to count. . . . There is a not inconsiderable amount of physical privation suffered by many people in this country, which is not physically necessary. The cause is very often that what might be the means of comfort is diverted to the purpose of maintaining a decent appearance, or even a show of luxury (VIII, 392).

In putting forth this notion, Veblen comes square around to private property, the central factor in both his analysis and that of Marx.

Human nature being what it is, the struggle of each to possess more than his neighbor is inseparable from the institution of private property. . . ; and the present growth of sentiment among the body of the people— who possess less—favors, in a vague way, a readjustment adverse to the interests of those who possess more, and adverse to the possibility of legitimately possessing or enjoying "more"; that is to say, the growth of sentiment favors a socialistic movement. . . . With private property, under modern conditions, this jealousy and unrest are unavoidable (VIII, 397).

But if the unrest is unavoidable, and if it "favors a socialistic movement," it does not follow that the movement will *result* in socialism. In this connection, the most significant reaction of industrial workers has been trade unionism. In all developed countries, as was true already in Veblen's time, socialist movements have also been associated with industrialism. What struck Veblen as most strategic in trade unionist and socialist developments, however, was their tendency to seek the material comforts of the "vested interests," and, with equal importance and emasculating effects, to spend some critical portion of their energies in the patriotic support of nationalism.

Veblen's essays on Marxism were written in the first years of this century. At that time the leading and most industrialized capitalist nations were Great Britain, Germany, and the United States. The workers' dissent in Great Britain was politically represented by a moderate socialist movement, the forerunner of the even more moderate present-day Labour Party. In the United States, there were also a moderate socialist group, pretty thoroughly rejected by industrial workers, and a distinctly radical, anarcho-syndicalist group known as the Industrial Workers of the World. The latter was brutally suppressed in the years of World War I and subsequently, not without the cooperation of the American Federation of Labor. The most widespread and influential socialist workers' political movement was in Germany, and this was also the most generally radical movement.

Veblen took the German Social Democrats as his focus in order to show that the kind of "rationality" posited by Marx was in a process of steady deterioration even in its strongest case. Briefly, there was neither immiserization nor class polarization but a steady growth of businesslike unionism and patriotism:

In Germany, as elsewhere, the growth of the capitalistic system presently brought on trade-unionism; that is to say, it brought on an organized attempt on the part of the workmen to deal with the questions of capitalistic production and distribution by business methods, to settle the problems of working-class employment and livelihood by a system of non-political, businesslike bargains. But the great point of all socialist aspiration and endeavor is the abolition of all business and all bargaining (VIII, 449).

Veblen goes on to point out that the reaction of the Social Democrats to this development was to change their (Marxian) theory—to abandon the notion of immiserization of the working class, and to substitute for that the idea that "every improvement in working-class conditions is to be counted as a gain for the revolutionary forces" (VIII, 450). In addition, in Germany as elsewhere, industrialism, far from reducing the size of the "middle class," encouraged a proliferation of functions (in trade and finance, e.g.) and an increase of those identifying their interests with the middle class. From Veblen's standpoint, this encouragement meant a strengthening of the ideology of the vested interests, most particularly that aspect centering on questions of nationalism.

German socialism, in the middle of the nineteenth century, was internationalist in outlook, "strongly averse to international jealousy and patriotic animosity, and . . . against armaments, wars, and dynastic aggrandisement" (VIII, 452). Thus, during the Franco-Prussian War, socialists in both France and Germany urged non-participation. The period after the 1870's was one of increasing nationalism and developing worldwide friction. The socialists in Germany had a choice: to become more, or to become less, radical. They chose the moderate path.

The socialist spokesmen have been continually on the defensive. They set out with a round opposition to any considerable military establishment, and have more and more apologetically continued to oppose any "undue" extension of the warlike establishments and warlike policy. But with the passage of time and the habituation to warlike politics and military discipline, the infection of jingoism had gradually permeated the body of Social Democrats, until they have now [1907] reached such a pitch of enthusiastic loyalty as they would not patiently hear a truthful characterization of. . . . The relative importance of the national and the international ideals in German socialist professions has been reversed since the seventies. . . . The Social Democrats have come to be German patriots first and socialists second, which comes to saying that they are a political party working for the maintenance of the existing order, with modifications (VIII, 453-54).

Before ten years had passed, German, French, and British socialists—if with momentary hesitation, and nostalgic soul-searching—were at each other's throats in supporting the national military efforts of World War I. Veblen's last words on future probabilities provide little cheer for those who would find agreeable the prospect of a militant, humanitarian, rational—or successful—socialist movement, gaining strength as industrialism proceeds through time:

> The imperial policy seems in a fair way to get the better of revolutionary socialism, not by repressing it, but by force of the discipline in imperialistic ways of thinking to which it subjects all classes of the population. How far a similar process of sterilization is under way, or is likely to overtake the socialist movement in other countries, is an obscure question to which the German object-lesson affords no certain answer (VIII, 456).

Marxian economic theory has two sides: scientific and propagandistic. Its propaganda impact, its ability to kindle and to sustain revolutionary movements, has been so substantial as to require no comment. Its scientific value has been mixed. Marx attempted to "lay bare the laws of motion of capitalist society." That attempt may be viewed from many sides, but here we may confine ourselves to only two. Marxian economic theory attempts to explain how capitalism works, and it attempts to forecast the long-run development and disruption of capitalism. In the first respect, by the questions he asked, and the "variables" and relationships he looked to, Marx did much to foster our understanding of important aspects of behavior under capitalist institutions. The second respect was the one focussed on most heavily by Veblen, and that was the Marxian theory of history. Theory may be tested in various ways. When it illuminates essentials and the relationships between them, it enables us to understand what might otherwise be unintelligible. It also provides, thereby, a guide for policy. If Marxian economic theory is not perfect in these respects, it is nonetheless possessed of many useful insights that persist to this day.

Marxism as a theory of history comes off less well. The test of a theory of history lies in its predictive value. Were Marxian theory correct, the most advanced industrial capitalist nations—Germany, France, Great Britain, the United States, and Japan, to select the most important—would surely by now have experienced revolutionary changes resulting in socialist regimes. There have of course been many modifications of "pure capitalism" in all the foregoing nations, many of them fostered by socialist groups. But whatever may be said of these changes, they do not come to what Marx had in mind when he predicted socialism as an outgrowth of industrial capitalism. Nor, it must be said, is the agitation for socialist institutions growing in the advanced countries. In all of them, rising levels of life, emulation, and patriotism have combined to produce what might at most be termed state capitalism, with a pronounced nationalistic orientation.

In this century, the nations that have experienced revolutions, or that face them, have been *seeking* industrialism, not *reacting* to it. What they have reacted to is some combination of the evils presumably produced by foreign economic and political domination, economic backwardness and poverty, indignity, and overall weakness. Such nations hold fiercely to the conviction that, through combining political independence with economic and social planning, they can and will eliminate the many causes and consequences of backwardness.

That, for such nations, the meaning of patriotism is expressed in hostility (or, at best, skepticism) toward the developed countries—whose aid they both need and feel entitled to, for both historical and current reasons—and that their ideologies are anticapitalist in a mild or strong degree, should occasion little surprise. It has frequently been pointed out that the class struggle envisaged by Marx is operating today between the rich and the poor nations, rather than (or at least much more than) as he expected, between workers and employers within the industrialized nations.

If these strictures on the validity of Marxian developmental theory are applicable, and they seem to be, the Marxian predictions have run aground principally on the shoals pointed to by Veblen: Marx's metaphysical preconceptions. Veblen had great respect for Marx's powerful mind, for the questions he asked, and for his methods of inquiry and analysis. However, although Marx appears as a giant among social scientists, he did not rise above *all* the preconceptions of his day. Neither, as will be discussed in Chapter 5, did Veblen.

Chapter 4

VEBLEN AND THE MAIN CURRENTS
OF THE TWENTIETH CENTURY

Veblen weighed the theorists of his day and found them wanting. When we weigh Veblen, what do we find? Our answer to this question will proceed along two different but related paths. In this chapter we shall examine some of Veblen's more interesting and important judgments and predictions and evaluate them against relevant historical events and processes. In the closing chapter we shall undertake an examination of the main components of Veblenian theory, in order to illuminate its strengths and weaknesses.

The twentieth century has no monopoly on economic and social change, violence, hope, or fear. All these are to be found scattered regularly throughout history. But it may at least be said that their scope and pace in this century exceed that of earlier times—or so, at least it seems. Future historians may characterize our century in any number of ways not presently foreseeable—as a century of progress or disaster, of beginnings or endings, among other possibilities—but those of us living in it are likely to make our characterizations in terms of those developments that have most affected us, filled us most with hope and well-being, desperation and misery. There have been many such developments; but surely on all lists there would occur the two world wars, the depression of the thirties, the spread of totalitarianism and conformity, the breakdown of colonialism, the gains in productivity and real income in the developed economies, and the emergence of

THORSTEIN VEBLEN

a military technology which must render either war or man obsolete.*

Veblen did not foresee each and every one of these developments jot and tittle; but he did capture what he called "the main drift" of this century, and he captured much of it in uncanny detail, as regards what happened, where, and in what manner. Underlying the main drift of the twentieth century have been those matters which most absorbed Veblen's energies: industrial technology, nationalism, capitalist institutions, social psychology, and the genetic process that results as these interact over time. In the next chapter we shall attempt a critical evaluation of Veblen's remarkable "record"—in no important degree approximated by any other American social scientist.

What concerned Veblen most in his last productive years was the probable course of development of the already advanced societies. Beginning in 1915 (with *Imperial Germany and the Industrial Revolution*) and ending in 1923 (with *Absentee Ownership*), Veblen never relaxed his focus on the prospects for cultural advance or retrogression, and of war and peace, as these would be determined by developments (principally) in Germany, Japan, and the United States.**

It may be said that once Veblen had begun to study Germany, it became an obsession with him. What he thought concerning Germany he generally applied to Japan as well. Considering that the emergence of fascism in Germany and Japan in the thirties, and the march into World War II led by them, was anticipated by Veblen as early as 1915, his obsession is understandable.

Veblen thought of Germany as the prime "disturber of the world's peace." The United States (or, more generally, "the

* Veblen's treatment of the questions of 1) colonialism, and 2) the Soviet Union is such as to make it seem least awkward to place them in an appendix to this chapter. Why this is so will be explained at that point.
** *The Higher Learning in America*, a witty and incisive view of American college and university life, although published in 1918, was written before 1905. *Essays in Our Changing Order*, published after Veblen's death, is a collection of articles which, with two unimportant exceptions, were written before 1923.

English-speaking peoples"), Veblen saw as most (but not very) likely to thwart the probabilities inherent in the German situation. Consequently, on the one hand he underlined the threat of Germany, and on the other assayed the contending possibilities in the United States, in a series of essays and books stretching over eight years. In his last book, concerned principally with the United States, Veblen gave up hope. Of the two major probabilities for America Veblen had set forth in *The Theory of Business Enterprise*—toward industrial democracy, *or* away from that and toward war—he had, by 1923, come down hard in expecting the latter. To comprehend Veblen's reasoning, we shall review his analysis 1) of Germany, as contained in *Imperial Germany*, and 2) of the factors making for war, as put forth in *The Nature of Peace*. The chapter will conclude with Veblen's view of the general drift in the United States, as seen in *Absentee Ownership*.

Veblen's analysis of modern Germany was written as World War I began. In it, the factors making for war and peace seldom were outside his focus. *Imperial Germany* undertakes to reveal the nature and force of the drives that brought Germany to a position of industrial strength combined with a persistent warlike stance. In *The Nature of Peace* (1917), Veblen's major theme was the necessity of defeating Germany completely in the ⌐ ¬, and of encouraging and allowing "the common man" to rule over a Germany with its fangs—the aligned military and economic interests—removed. Failing this, Veblen expected that Germany (in alliance with Japan)* would once again "disturb the peace," steered by an aggressive feudal ideology powered with the latest in modern technology. The reasoning underlying this position contained useful insights into the process of economic development, but Veblen was more intent on what supported his dire warning to those who placed peace and democracy at the head of their list of social values.

At the center of Veblen's analysis of German development is the notion that "a given technological system will

---

* An unusual alliance to think of at that time, with Japan a member of the Allies. See V, 82-83.

have an economic value and a cultural incidence on a community which takes it over ready-made, different from the effects it has already wrought in the community from which it is taken over and in which it has cumulatively grown to maturity . . ." (IV, 88).

In elaboration of this thesis, Veblen compared the industrialization processes of England and Germany. What John U. Nef has called "the first industrial revolution" occurred in England in the sixteenth and seventeenth centuries. At the beginning of that period, England was "in cultural arrears" (IV, 91) as compared with the rest of Europe (including most of Germany). Because of its insular location, its comparative weakness, and its internal social situation, England remained *relatively* secluded from the political, military, and religious disturbances that for so long rocked Europe. While Europe fought and bled and wasted its resources in dynastic pursuits, England "borrowed and assimilated processes, workmen, and methods" from the then economically more advanced Continent. England steadily became more of a commercial, and less of a dynastic, society—most obviously manifest in her middle-class revolution stretching from 1640 to 1688 and culminating in the triumph of parliamentary rule.

In that process, and building from it, the principal features of the natural rights philosophy emerged, against a background of pre-industrial, capitalistically-motivated agriculture, trade, and industry. As the ideology of a commercial society took hold in England, the discipline of the medieval, subservient, military outlook was weakened. England became the home of a philosophy of self-interest and utilitarianism. Whatever might be said of such a viewpoint when later faced with the imperatives of modern industry, it contributed to a skeptical view of the use of state power. As Veblen put it, "The British subject's loyalty to the reigning monarch or to the crown is conditioned on the serviceability of such allegiance to his own material interests. A loyalty which raises the question What for? comes far short of the feudalistic ideal and of that spirit of enthusiastic abnegation that has always been the foundation of a prosperous dynastic state" (IV, 103).

Slowly and steadily, in a manner too complicated to be related here, England developed interrelated agricultural, trading, industrial, and financial activities to the point where the technology of the classic industrial revolution burst forth, much as a river that grows and swells and finally overflows its banks. The banks that overflowed in England were those of the institutions developed to accord with the pre-modern economic situation—centering on the system of economic individualism and competition, the rights of ownership and the aims of pecuniary enterprise. These latter made up the institutional framework within which modern industry had to function. But, according to Veblen, "that broad fringe of usages, conventions, vested rights, canons of equity and propriety, that are no part of the new state of the industrial arts . . . , have the effect of hindrances to the working of the industrial system, or of deductions from its net efficiency" (IV, 121).

Consequently, the British (in 1915) "are paying the penalty for having been thrown into the lead and so having shown the way" (IV, 132). Veblen did not mean to say that the British were badly off in absolute terms. It was a problem, rather, of what "the British might be doing if it were not for the restraining dead hand of their past achievement, and by further contrast, latterly, with what the newcome German people are doing by use of the English technology lore" (IV, 132).

The economic development of Germany in the late nineteenth century can be understood only when it is viewed as an integral part of the growth of the German Empire. This latter process, like the former, was led by the Prussians, in a series of connected steps having their beginning in the wake of the Napoleonic Wars. Economically, the first major step was the creation of a customs union, the Zollverein, eliminating tariff barriers between participating German states and placing a common tariff wall around them against non-members (much in the manner of today's European Common Market). Next was the development of a modern transportation system, based upon a unified rail network. Taken together, the Zollverein and the railroad had many effects, not least of which were the broadening of markets and the feasibility of modern industrial technology in Germany. Rapid economic development began in the years surrounding 1850; by 1871, the year when Empire was proclaimed, Germany was well on the road to full-scale industrialization. By then it had also become a first-rate military power, as revealed in the Franco-Prussian War, and a power whose aggressive aims were not to be satisfied by that serio-comic triumph.

What made modern Germany the most volatile of European nations was neither its political nor its economic situation taken separately, but the combination of the two, its historical background, and its role as a late-comer in the scramble for power. Its persisting medieval outlook, combined with a powerful technology, made Germany the leading candidate for the role of "disturber of the peace"—a role shared with Japan in the latter's hemisphere.*

Veblen's explanation of the aggressive propensities of modern Germany rests on historical conditioning, rather than on any exceptional characteristics of German leaders—who were leaders "not because these personages were exceptions, but because they were not" (IV, 153)—or any unique racial traits:

In respect of the stable characteristics of race heredity the German people do not differ in any sensible or consistent manner from the neighboring peoples; whereas in the character of their past habituation—in their cultural scheme—as well as in respect of the circumstances to which they have latterly been exposed, their case is at least in some degree peculiar. It is in the matter of received habits of thought—use and wont—and in the conditions that have further shaped their scheme of use and wont in the recent past, that the population of this country differs from the population of Europe at large (IV, 6).

* "The Opportunity of Japan" (XI, 248-66) succinctly presents Veblen's analysis for that country; in doing so, it serves as an indirect and shorthand statement of the German case. Like *Imperial Germany,* it was written in 1915.

What characteristics of Germany's "past habituation and received habits of thought" are relevant here? And from the congeries of three hundred odd petty principalities making up "Germany" as the nineteenth century began, how, asks Veblen, explain that it was Prussia that typified Germany as the century ended; and how explain the Prussian mentality itself?

Many a well-meaning apologist for the German people . . . has been at pains to recall that Prussia is not Germany, and the German spirit of the south especially, in the traditional seats of German culture, is of a very different and more genial kind than that which animates the community of Junkers in the north; these Germans of the south and west, from Austria all across to the confines of the Low Countries, have, it is said, . . . shown an inclination to live and let live; or as seen from the higher levels of Prussian efficiency, they have been a slack-twisted lot (IV, 154).

Veblen's explanation for the aggressiveness of Prussia lies in the centuries-long history of its involvement in offensive and defensive warfare, and protracted periods of "ruthless exploitation, terror, disturbances, reprisals, servitude and gradual habituation to settled allegiance, irresponsible personal rule, and peaceable repression" (IV, 157). While England, in the late medieval and early modern periods, was moving away from dynastic rule and toward a commercial, parliamentary society, the areas of Prussian hegemony were, in these terms, retrogressing. What in the thirteenth and fourteenth centuries had been a lively agricultural and trading area, in the fifteenth century took a turn toward harsh medieval agrarian institutions—from freedom to serfdom, briefly—and the subordination of commercialism to a dynastic, princely militarism. The disastrous point of no return in this long process was reached in the decimating and devastating Thirty Years' War. The political, military, and economic consequences of that catastrophe were in all respects retrogressive, and they were to hold Germany prisoner for another two hundred years—at least. They were also the foundations upon which the new Germany was to be constructed.

The Thirty Years' War would not have taken place had Germany been surrounded by peaceable neighbors; nor was it only Prussia, of the German states, that was involved in the process just outlined. It was not Veblen's point that Germany was alone among the European powers in its leaning toward aggressive militarism, nor that Prussia was alone among the German states in being so inclined.* It was to Veblen a matter of degree as between all these, and a matter of habituation, circumstance, and alternative possibilities. What swam on the surface in Germany was barely submerged in the other Great Powers; and a similar relationship held as between Prussia and the other German states.

> But while the Imperial State and its policy are of Prussian pedigree, it is easy to over-rate that fact. It should be called to mind that while the subjects of the south-German states . . . were disinclined to the Prussian rule and the Prussian aims, the population of these states have after all . . . passed under the Prussian hegemony and accepted the drift of Prussian political aims somewhat easily. In point of fact there was not much of anything available in the way of public sentiment and national aspiration in these non-Prussian states, else than a dilute form of the same thing. Their earlier experience had run along the same general lines, except for a certain lack of success attending their princely policies. . . . It is not as if the Prussian system had been imposed on an English-speaking people, e.g., with inbred notions of popular autonomy and private initiative (IV, 212-13).

The Germany that emerged from the Napoleonic Wars was backward economically, but it was so constituted that it

---

* Indeed, a more plausible view would argue that from at least the sixteenth century it was France (and its varying allies) that was the prime disturber of Europe's, and most particularly, Germany's peace; that, furthermore, the fragmentation of Germany into a patchwork of petty dynastic states was a cardinal aim of French policy.

could move swiftly once a process of unification and modernization was begun. The crazy-quilt of German principalities had the virtues of its defects, as Veblen would say, in that the multiplication of political units required a vast, if duplicative, bureaucracy. Training for and manning of this bureaucracy produced what was probably the best-educated population in all Europe; it also instilled a "bureaucratic" outlook in Germany, which was later to be applied with positive effect in the running of the highly organized German industrial society. Secondly, the economic backwardness of Germany (by the eighteenth century) was the backwardness not of stagnation but of a pre-industrial technology. Germany was a nation of numerous and active traders and handicraftsmen, of substantial experience and pronounced skills. These qualities were easily translated into those needed for an industrial economy, and their existence does much to explain the rapidity of Germany's transition from a backward to a leading industrial economy within the space of two generations.

As the German industrialization process began, it was guided, wrote Veblen, by "the ancient cameralistic aim of making the most of the nation's resources for the dynastic purposes of the State" (IV, 175). That is, German industrial development was, relative to the British or the American, much less a matter of uncorrelated individuals pursuing their own pecuniary interests. German businessmen sought, and made, profits, of course; but they acted within (and helped to create) a framework of national policy at once more self-conscious, more exacting, and more coherent than had hitherto accompanied the industrialization process.*

* "Cameralism" may be read as the German version of "mercantilism": i.e., a set of policies promoting the mutual development of state power and private advantage. The mercantilist period in England ended as the industrial period began—it was against a dying mercantilism that Adam Smith wrote—but it carried into and expanded in the German industrialization process. It may be noted in passing that France (except for a decade or two) remained "mercantilist" throughout her history, also, but that before World War I France gained less from a thoroughgoing industrialization process than from bountiful natural resources and a rich empire.

As such, in Veblen's view, much of the waste of the purer enterprise system was avoided.

Both the structure of German production and the pattern of ownership and control were, by comparison with the British situation, lopsided: Germany's productive structure leaned heavily in the direction of heavy industry (metallurgy, mining, machinery, shipbuilding, chemicals), well-designed for rapid industrialization and military strength; the pattern of control, which was concentrated and interlocked, rested on the corporation, the cartel, and the large industrial bank. The peasant, unlike his English counterpart, was maintained, as was the large farmer, the Junker.* But the Junker was more than a farmer, and the peasant played a role going beyond the raising of crops. The Junker was at the center of power in Germany, in politics and in the military, and his viewpoint was integrated into the policies directing the path of the German economy—with the insured support of a reactionary peasantry.

Germany's central location and poor (natural) resource endowment help to explain the pace and direction of her development. Germany's location, devoid of effective natural barriers, has historically made of it some combination of highway and battleground. But modern German leaders had a more enticing vision: Germany as the industrial and military hub of Europe. Such ambitions were not unique in Europe's history. Added impetus was given to them in Germany by the problems connected with her natural resources.

As is well-known, the Fatherland is not at all specially fortunate in natural resources of the class that count toward modern industry. As regards mineral resources Germany has a decided advantage in one item of potash

---

* More accurately, inefficient agriculture was maintained. A surplus farm population developed in the generation around mid-century which, together with political unrest, led (generally) to emigration of South and West Germans to the U.S.A., and of East Germans to the factories. After the late 1870's, the agricultural situation was "stabilized" by a series of tariff measures protecting both agriculture and industry.

alone. The iron and coal deposits are well enough, but can by no means be counted as better than second best, in point of quality, location, or abundance (IV, 180).

And much the same may be said of forest, fishery, and soil resources, Veblen added. Moreover, the best and most strategic of Germany's resources lay at her periphery; i.e., adjoining the borders of her enemies.

These, and matters mentioned earlier, led to a set of economic policies making it difficult to know where military considerations left off and economic considerations began. If Germany's rail system was well-designed for industrialization, it was even better suited to provide the means of swift travel to the borders, for either offensive or defensive purposes. If natural resources scarcity led to the search for *ersatz* (substitute) products, and the application of science to industry, it also led to a precocious chemical and explosives industry and aggressive attempts to guarantee sources of supply (Alsace-Lorraine ranking neither earliest nor least among the successful attempts). And, if Germany's industrial growth and efficiency were, by historical standards, spectacular, it was also true, according to Veblen, that Germany took the lead

in the application of . . . technological knowledge to what may be called the industrial arts of war, with at least no less zeal and no less effect than in its utilization in the arts of peace. . . . [Since 1890], preparation for war on a large scale has been going forward unremittingly, and at a constantly accelerating rate, whether as measured in terms of absolute magnitude or as measured in terms of expenditure per capita of population, or of percentages of current income or of accumulated wealth, or as compared with the corresponding efforts of neighboring states (IV, 256-57).

Veblen, it must be emphasized, did not view the outbreak of World War I as the result of an evil genius possessed solely by Germany. Veblen saw the *relatively* peaceable qualities of the British and the French as having reached their heights in the third quarter of the nineteenth century and as having been on the decline since that time. The ensuing general movement toward a more belligerent posture among nations was encouraged by a technology which tended "to neutralize the geographical quarantine which had hedged about these communities that were inclined to let well enough alone" (V, 17). The improving technology of warfare, the scramble for colonies, and the increasingly swift means of transportation and communication, among other things, combined so that

> the fear of aggression . . . came definitively to take the place of international good will and became the chief motive in public policy, so fast and so far as the state of the industrial arts continued to incline the balance of advantage to the side of the aggressor. All of which served greatly to strengthen the hands of those statesmen who, by interest or temperament, were inclined to imperialistic enterprise. Since that period all armament has been conventionally accounted defensive, and all statesmen have professed that the common defense is their chief concern (V, 18).

The outbreak of war was the result of interacting national needs and ambitions. Veblen saw that the special role attributable to Germany was not that of a devil among angels; rather it had "the distinction of taking the lead and forcing the pace" (V, 20). Veblen viewed the situation before World War I as a room filled with powder kegs, with all the Great Powers holding matches. Whatever the protestations of peaceful intentions may have been or from whatever source, Veblen concluded that "it was not necessary formally to desire the war in order to bring it to a head, if only care was taken to make the preparations so complete as to make war unavoidable" (IV, 258-59).

As Veblen concluded *Imperial Germany*, he contemplated the consequences of World War I, and the final pages of that book link with the opening pages of *The Nature of*

Peace. In 1915, Veblen expected Germany to lose the war, because in the later stages of her arms preparations she had been followed by the other Great Powers, whose combined industrial and military strength would prove too much for Germany. But the prospect that Germany would lose the war did little to assuage Veblen's gloomy view of the future, for two reasons. The first was that

> whether the Imperial State wins or loses in the contest for the hegemony, the movement of cultural reversion for which in substance it is contending stands to gain at least to the extent of a substantial, though presumably temporary, impairment and arrest of Western civilization at large (IV, 271).

Secondly, Veblen was not at all confident that the "impairment and arrest of Western civilization" would be temporary.

Whether or not the world would recover from the war and progress toward the civilization made posssible by the growth of science and technology, he knew, would be determined by the nature of the peace settlement and the subsequent institutional turn of the advanced industrial societies. In brief, Veblen argued that the peace settlement must neutralize Germany, in both its military and non-military potential for predatory behavior; that a "pacific league of nations" must be formed to keep the peace; that this would require substantial institutional modifications toward industrial democracy within all nations; and that, finally, the lead in this respect must be taken by "the English-speaking peoples" —chiefly by the United States. The alternatives to this were deadly: the re-emergence of an even more dangerous militarism in a totalitarian Germany (joined by a Japanese twin), and similarly dangerous, but not identical, tendencies in the other industrial nations.

The Nature of Peace is an inquiry into "the nature, causes and consequences of . . . [the] preconception favoring peace, and the circumstances that make for a contrary preconception in favor of war" (V, 3). The elements of Veblen's analysis of war and peace have been touched upon in earlier pages. Its hard core is composed of "the nature and uses of patriotism," the meaning of nationalism in the modern world, and the relationships between these, business enterprise, and the modern technology.

The patriotic spirit had its origins in man's dim beginnings, declared Veblen, when hunting and standing with one's tribe or clan to fight outsiders were the prime means of survival and material well-being. With the passage of millennia and the improvement of technology, predatory behavior persisted, even though no longer essential to material well-being. Political and social organization changed substantially over time, e.g., from clan to nation, but as hunting was replaced by agriculture, trade, and industry, the martial spirit remained, albeit in a fancier set of uniforms.

The reasons for the "conservation of the archaic trait" of patriotism were at the heart of Veblen's *Theory of the Leisure Class*. They revolve around the political and social position held by the nucleus of the leisure class, its actual or imputed military prowess historically, and the emulative inclinations of the common man.

> The patriotic spirit is a spirit of emulation, evidently, at the same time that it is emulation shot through with a sense of solidarity. It belongs under the general caption of sportsmanship, rather than workmanship. Now, any enterprise in sportsmanship is bent on an invidious success, which must involve as its major purpose the defeat and humiliation of some competitor, whatever else may be composed in its aim . . . ; and the emulative spirit that comes under the head of patriotism commonly, if not invariably, seeks this differential advantage by injury of the rival rather than by an increase of home-bred well-being (V, 33).

The weight given to habituation by Veblen enabled him to see patriotism maintained at a fever pitch in late-coming industrial countries such as dynastic Germany and Japan, and as having been relatively subordinated in countries long exposed to the machine technology and money-making, such as Great Britain and the United States. And, although all nations, by their existence, inculcate and require "the martial spirit"—"The most peaceable governmental policy of which Christendom has experience is a policy of 'watchful waiting,' with a jealous eye to the emergence of any occasion for national resentment. . . ." (V, 7)—differences of degree between nations in this respect, Veblen knew, are crucial in the precarious balance between war and peace.

The principal factors giving rise to these differences are the level of technology and the extent to which a given population has been exposed to the "matter-of-fact" habituation of an industrial society. Veblen did not have a simple view of the relationship between technological development and the erosion of the "archaic traits" of nationalism and patriotism, such that as the former grew the latter would decline and disappear. His theory posits alternation and tension—in effect, a race—between the life-giving influence of productive industry and the death-dealing influence of predatory nationalism. But the "race" does not have a prescribed distance or a fixed finish line. Veblen envisaged a process where the primacy of either the productive or the predatory propensities of man was temporary; where each dominated over time only at the expense of the other, in a situation of mutual incompatibility; where each had only a limited time in which to prevail. Veblen was far from optimistic that the beneficial possibilities of industrialism could be realized without the elimination of all vestiges of the patriotic spirit. And, Veblen asserted, were the predatory inclination to triumph, it must over time cripple the functioning and the further development of science and technology.

This analysis may be illuminated further by contrasting Veblen's views of the development of Germany and Japan, on the one hand, and the United States, on the other. The aggressive inclinations of Germany and Japan have been pointed to earlier. But Veblen did not expect that these inclinations were or could be permanent characteristics of those nations. They were a holdover from the pre-industrial histories of these countries; and there was a limited time period in which dynastic inclinations would be able to harness industrial power to fulfill its objectives. Viewing Japan in this light, Veblen issued a warning that became a prophecy:

> . . . if this new found [industrial] efficiency is to serve the turn for the dynastic aggrandisement of Japan, it must be turned to account before the cumulatively accelerating rate of institutional deterioration overtakes and neutralizes the cumulatively declining rate of gain in material efficiency; which should, humanly speaking, mean that Japan must strike, if at all, within the effective lifetime of the generation that is now coming to maturity (XI, 266).

The "institutional deterioration" of which Veblen speaks was at full gallop in Japan in the late twenties and early thirties, as labor and socialist organizations and business groups came into increasing conflict with each other, the military, and the state. The conflict was resolved by a more intimate alliance between military and business interests, which then "became" the state. The product of this alliance was Japanese fascism. It in turn suppressed civil liberties and the labor movement in Japan, and yielded the war that Veblen expected—"within the effective lifetime of the generation [then: 1915] coming to maturity."

Germany industrialized before World War I. Growing along with its powerful and well-controlled economy was a set of repressive social institutions that hindered improvements in the economic and political well-being of the industrial population. Fighting against this in Germany was the largest and most radical working-class movement in Europe.* With Germany's defeat in the war, it would have been "natural" for Germany to have fallen under the control of

---

* A movement that, as was pointed out earlier, was fast shedding its most radical features as World War I approached. After the war, the socialist movement in Germany had split into the moderate Social Democratic wing and the radical Communist wing. These two groups warred against each other as much as against their common enemies, down to and even beyond Hitler's capture of power.

"common men." It seemed, for a while, that this would be the outcome. The Weimar Republic of the twenties was, at least in appearance and rhetoric, the farthest "left" government of western Europe; also, in the late twenties, Germany was the center of intellectual activity in the West, extending through the range of arts and sciences. But this genial political and cultural situation proved to be superficial. Underneath were continual rumbles of strife, military ambition, and hatred.

The structure and control of the German economy was left predominantly untouched by military defeat, except that control became even more concentrated after the war than it had been earlier. Patriotism, far from decreasing, became virulent. Germany, as Veblen saw matters, had been defeated at the wrong time, and the years to follow would be the worse for it.

> . . . in the absence of American intervention the hostilities would have been continued until the German nation had been exhausted. . . , which would have demoralized and discredited the rule of privilege and property in the Fatherland to such effect that the control of affairs would have passed out of the hands of the kept classes. The outcome should then have been an effective liquidation of the old order and the installation of something like an industrial democracy resting on other ground than privilege and property, instead of the camouflage of a *pro forma* liquidation . . . (XI, 423-24).*

---

* To which Veblen added, a few pages later: "Even if the Americans had not come in and upset the fighting-balance, the European statesmen might have seen their way to much the same sort of negotiated peace, with much the same view to renewed hostilities at a later date" (XI, 426). This was written in 1919. It should be pointed out that Veblen supported American intervention in the war in 1915, because of his deeply-held conviction that Germany, and what it stood for, must be contained. In 1922, Veblen was to deplore (in the essay "Dementia Præcox," in XI) the dangerous consequences for American thinking induced by her participation. But that was after the failure of a meaningful peace settlement of the sort he had hoped America might help create.

Given the persistence of the old Germany in fact, if not in form, the rule of the irrational, and especially of the patriotic spirit, would triumph in Germany and elsewhere, Veblen declared:

. . . these peoples of the Empire and its allies, as well as their enemies in the great war, will necessarily come out of their warlike experience in a more patriotic and vindictive frame of mind than that in which they entered on this adventure. Fighting makes for malevolence. The war itself is to be counted as a set-back. A very large proportion of those who have lived through it will necessarily carry a warlike bent through life (V, 195).

Postwar Germany was a potential battleground between two German forces: those proposing to modify seriously or sweep away the pre-war structure, and those proposing to maintain it intact. In the former camp were the mutually hostile Social Democrats and the Communists, whose combined forces could (but did not) command a majority of the popular vote in Germany by 1930. On the other side were the combined forces of the German army, large and small agricultural interests, and the interlocked trading, industrial and financial powers. The struggle for power in Germany, more so than elsewhere, was to be one of extremes. It was this tension Veblen referred to when he made the sardonic judgment that the Germans were

newcomers whose scheme of life has not yet been made over in the image of that [modern] culture into which they are moving by force of unavoidable habituation,— unavoidable except by a precipitate retreat into that more archaic phase of western civilization out of which they have latterly been escaping.

It is not yet too late, perhaps. They may yet be able to effect such a retreat by recourse to so drastic a reaction in their civil and political institutions as will offset, presently neutralize, and eventually dispel the effects wrought by habituation to the ways and means of modern industry and the exact sciences (IV, 236-37).

The "drastic reaction in civil and political institutions" was to appear in Germany in the form of Nazism some eighteen years later.

Of the abiding questions of this century, one of the more unsettling has to do with the role played by the western democracies as Japanese and German totalitarianism took shape and finally pushed to war.* The explanation for this rôle requires that we turn our attention to the tensions growing within industrial capitalist societies, and the bearing of these on the function of nationalism and patriotism in "modern" societies. Certain relevant aspects of these relationships have been commented on in earlier chapters. Here we shall extend the argument by looking at the situation prevailing in the twenties, and our focus will be restricted to America.

Veblen thought that the maintenance of peace, once achieved, would depend upon the "pacific nations"—most importantly, the Allies. In that group, Great Britain and the United States were the key members; the former because her position, her strength, and her empire made her indispensable (V, 296), and America because a league to keep the peace was indispensable to her ultimate well-being. This latter judgment might be made of Great Britain and others, of course; but Veblen thought that America's historic isolation from international strife might lead her to see this more easily: that Great Britain was too much of "an interested party" in European affairs to be trusted. However, even as he wrote these lines, Veblen had been virtually drained of hope that America would play the requisite role.

The bases for Veblen's skepticism regarding the United States we shall examine shortly. The need for active American participation in the keeping of the peace was simply that

---

* Italy became a fascist nation earlier than Japan or Germany and was aligned with them in war as in mood. Space does not permit, nor does our present focus require, a discussion of Italy. There were important differences between Italian fascism and that of Germany and Japan, and there were important similarities. The genetic analysis employed by Veblen sheds much light on both.

a league of "pacific" nations without the United States would be a case of the old dog up to his old tricks in a different guise.

> With or without the adherence of America, the pacific nations of Europe will doubtless endeavor to form a league or alliance designed to keep the peace. If America does not come into the arrangement it may well come to nothing much more than a further continued defensive alliance of the belligerent nations now opposed to the German coalition . . . in which case it will necessarily be transient, perhaps ephemeral . . . (V, 297).

What Veblen thought necessary "to keep the peace" was a gradual disappearance of the trappings of nationalism—through disarmament, "the neutralization of citizenship" (V, 205 ff.), and the elimination of economic nationalism at home and abroad.* It was the exacting nature of these conditions that led Veblen to be skeptical regarding the necessary role of the United States. So skeptical was he in this critical respect that we need not examine his strictures regarding Great Britain and France.

The United States did not, of course, join the League of Nations, despite Wilson's efforts to that end and the early popularity of the League in American public opinion. Veblen foresaw (in 1917) the ultimate weakness of the League and Wilson's defeat in America. His reasons for expecting this outcome centered on the aims and the power of business, and their interest in perpetuating the very things an effective League would terminate:

> The business interests have much to say in the counsels of the Americans, and these business interests look to short-term gains—American business interests particular-

---

* Veblen's distrust and detestation of nationalism in whatever form it might manifest itself should by now be clear; the most succinct statement of his position may be found in "The Passing of National Frontiers" (XI, 383-90). *The Nature of Peace* may be thought of as a tract against nationalism.

ly—to be derived from the country's necessities. It is likely to appear that the business interests, through representatives in Congress and elsewhere, will disapprove of any peace compact that does not involve an increase of the national armament and a prospective demand for munitions and an increased expenditure of the national funds (V, 297).

Veblen, it will be recalled, classed business enterprise as a modern form of predatory behavior. One of his recurring themes was the attempt of the businessman "to get something for nothing"; i.e., at the expense of the community: ". . . the arts of business are arts of bargaining, effrontery, make-believe, and are directed to the gain of the businessman at the cost of the community, at large and in detail" (X, 107).

To Veblen it was axiomatic that businessmen would support anything promising gain, and not stick at activities that were harmful to the society: "the common good is [not] a business proposition" (*Ibid.*). Consequently, the political weight of business would be placed behind the very developments that Veblen thought must be curtailed—e.g., tariffs and arms production. This action would substantially reduce the possibility that America would become an effective force making for peace in the world. What business wants, business gets.

Veblen assumed this outcome to be so, even if popular feeling might run in a direction opposite from business interests; for popular feeling could be led to turn in a direction more suited to the occasion. Although Americans were habituated by long exposure to conditions of modern life, and were largely exempt from a feudal background and outlook, the virtual enshrinement of the businessman meant that politics would be shaped in his image. In this regard, the few years just following World War I were critical.

Compared to others, the generations of Americans living between the Civil War and World War I had been a pacific people. Of course, Indians were subdued, even brutally; the "splendid little war" with Spain provided excitement (and territory); and the drums of patriotism were pounded hard during the World War. But if Americans had a penchant for violence, they leaned more toward individualistic displays than the concerted heroism of international wars. So it seemed, at least, half a century ago. The mood of Americans as the war ended was largely one of revulsion, with a bias toward pacifism—for a while. If the war had encouraged pacifism in some, it had also brought out the bellicose in other Americans. The Russian Revolution gave those who sought one a starting point for the spread of fear, which soon took on dimensions that led America toward political repression and hysteria. As Veblen wrote:

The current situation in America [1922] is by way of being something of a psychiatrical clinic. . . . Perhaps the commonest and plainest evidence of . . . unbalanced mentality is to be seen in a certain fearsome and feverish credulity with which a large proportion of Americans are affected. As contrasted with their state of mind before the war, they are predisposed to believe in footless outrages and odious plots and machinations—"treasons, stratagems, and spoils." They are readily provoked to a headlong intolerance, and resort to unadvised atrocities as a defense against imaginary evils. There is a visible lack of composure and logical coherence, both in what they will believe and in what they are ready to do about it (XI, 429-30).

The foregoing is from the article "Dementia Praecox," written at a time when the Ku Klux Klan was under revival, the American Legion in its lusty infancy, the "Secret Service kept faithfully on the job of making two suspicions grow where one grew before" (XI, 432), and when traditional civil liberties seemed all but suspended. It was a time of hysteria whose targets were the "Bolshevik," the alien, the anarchist; but the practical effect of this hysteria was to weaken trade unions, socialist and pacifist groups, and to harass emigrants.

Under cover of it all the American profiteers have diligently gone about their business of getting something for nothing at the cost of all concerned, while popular attention has been taken up with the maudlin duties of civil and religious intolerance. The Republic has come through this era of spiritual dilapidation with an unbalanced budget and an increased armament by use of which to "safeguard American interests"—that is to say, negotiate profitable concessions for American oil companies—a system of passports, deportations, and restricted immigration, and a Legion of veterans organized for a draft on the public funds and the cultivation of warlike distemper. Unreflecting patriotic flurry has become a civic virtue (XI, 432).

The growth of "patriotic flurry" coincided with a shift of the pace and direction of the American economy. The shift had barely begun before the war; it was pronounced in the twenties. It involved changes in the structure both of control and of production, and, as well, associated changes in the general quality of life. It was a period when already big business grew to giant size; when financial manipulation and feverish speculation—perhaps the epitome of "getting something for nothing"—became an integral and even admirable activity for a large number of Americans; when mass production of consumer durables became a fundamental feature of the economy; and when, to support the latter, the manifest possibilities of persuasion and credit-buying came to be a major prop of the American economy. It was in this period, too, that government on all levels was administered by men whose devotion to business principles could not be questioned—Harding, Coolidge, and Hoover stand as symbols of the era.

The twenties have gone down in history as the "prosperity decade"; the thirties became the "depression decade." For the latter to have followed the former suggests that it was a product of the problems created, or left unsolved, in the former. These problems were anticipated by Veblen in *The*

Theory of Business Enterprise; they were witnessed by him as he wrote *Absentee Ownership*.

It will be recalled that in the *Theory* Veblen had argued that the further industrialization of the United States must yield a growth of industrial democracy, or turn to a future of stagnation, mixed with conspicuous consumption, armaments, and waste. The "red scare" of the twenties emasculated any forces that might have fought effectively for industrial democracy in that decade. The economic and political power of business, always great, was enhanced in the twenties. Not without a sedulous public relations campaign to that end, business gained a place in the hearts of its countrymen not dreamed of by the early "captains of industry"—certainly not by Commodore Vanderbilt in his "the public be damned!"

In the popular mind, the American economy took on the nature of a vast cornucopia, created by businessmen, with the function of pouring forth endless well-being. But this was not the popular mind of the farmers, the coal miners, the textile workers, or the railroad men—to mention only those experiencing the greatest difficulties in the twenties. They were the hardest hit; but what was obviously a period of trouble for those in the recognizably "sick" industries was something less than prosperity for workers in general, especially after 1925. By 1928, it has been estimated, American industry was on the average operating with something like thirty per cent excess capacity. There are no reliable unemployment statistics for the twenties, but conservative estimates place the average annual unemployment of the civilian labor force at five per cent.

Despite these signs of trouble, and more yet to come, the mood of the nation was optimistic. As late as 1929 it was the overwhelming opinion of economists, businessmen, and publicists that America had found the keys to permanent prosperity. Veblen's position stood in stark contrast. He recognized the uses to which advertising and salesmanship could be put in stimulating consumption; he also recognized that this could be best accomplished in a setting of controlled markets, based upon some mixture of collusion, mergers, protective tariffs, and inflated capital values. These he took to be the prime prospects for the economy in 1904; by 1923 he was able to see his expectations validated in the world about him. Veblen's general framework for analyzing the kind of economy America had in the twenties has been set forth in Chapter 2. Some of his direct observations in the twenties may add body to that framework.

Veblen's comments on the world of advertising antedate by decades today's recognition of the arts of hidden persuaders:

> . . . the technicians in charge of this work, as also the skilled personnel of the working-force [of advertising], are by way of being experts and experimenters in applied psychology, with a workmanlike bent in the direction of what may be called creative psychiatry. Their day's work will necessarily run on the creative guidance of habit and bias, by recourse to shock effects, tropismatic reactions, animal orientation, forced movements, fixation of ideas, verbal intoxication. It is a trading on that range of human infirmities which blossom in devout observances and bear fruit in the psychopathic wards (X, 307).

In the *Theory of Business Enterprise* Veblen had emphasized the factors for coalition and merger, and the transformation of the "captains of industry" into the "captains of finance." By 1923, this feature was well-established in the economy, and was for Veblen its strategic center. Investigations in the thirties were to show the key role played by two hundred dominant non-financial corporations, a handful of financial "interest groups," and the financial jiggery-pokery and resulting economic precariousness of the twenties. Veblen's characterization of this situation, as he saw it in 1923, is worth quoting at length:

> . . . there has presently emerged the new order of collusive moderation under the administrative guidance of the One Big Union of the Interests. Concert and mutual accommodation in the conduct of this industrial business is effectually dictated not by the technical re-

quirements of industry but by considerations of finance, with a view to mutual financial benefits, by financial concessions and alliances, under pressure of financial necessity.

Financial peace and stability is a matter of the first consequence to the Interests, and to all those who are concerned in the business of capitalized credits. The fabric of credit and capitalization is essentially a fabric of concerted make-believe resting on the routine credulity of the business community at large. It is therefore conditioned on the continued preservation of the prevalent credulity in a state of unimpaired tensile strength, which calls for eternal vigilance on the part of its keepers. The fabric, therefore, is always in a state of unstable equilibrium, liable to derangement and extensive disintegration in case of an appreciable disturbance at any critical point, with unhappy consequences for the business of capitalization and overhead charges . . . ; it is all a confidence game—in the blameless sense of the phrase . . . (X, 383-84).

Veblen assumed depression to be the normal condition in a business-enterprise economy, to be relieved in periods of excitation caused by stimuli not intrinsic to the system (e.g., war, expansion abroad, etc.). He also assumed that the "natural" tendency of the business community was to act so as to inflate capital values, and to attempt their maintenance at inflated levels by restricted production, market control, and salesmanship. Depending upon whether their attempts to control the economy would succeed or not, Veblen expected either some degree of stagnation (with intermittent expansion), or "derangement"; i.e., crisis and sharp contraction. However, Veblen did not have an adequately worked out theory of employment and business fluctuations. He appreciated only the negative aspects of modern financial institutions; he had the beginnings of a theory of consumer demand, but nothing more; and he tended either to overestimate or underestimate the relationship between market control and the functioning of the economy. All these limitations (and more to be explored in the next chapter) prevented Veblen from achieving a full understanding of what lay ahead in the decade or so to follow *Absentee Ownership*. But he did not fail to see in general terms the degree of disaster to which the economy could be brought by what he considered to be its basic characteristics. In this respect he stood very much alone among his American colleagues:

> For the immediate future the prospect appears to offer a fuller confirmation in the faith that business principles answer all things. The outlook should accordingly be that the businesslike control of the industrial system in detail should presently reach, if it has not already reached, and should speedily pass beyond that critical point of chronic derangement in the aggregate beyond which a continued pursuit of the same strategy on the same businesslike principles will result in a progressively widening margin of deficiency in the aggregate material output and a progressive shrinkage of the available means of life (X, 445).

Those are the last words of *Absentee Ownership*. They have been construed by some as fitting closely what was to begin in 1929; by others, they are seen as a statement so general as to lack useful meaning.

Veblen's assumption that the prospect was for "business principles to be the answer for all things" meant that the hopes for beneficial change, and the hopes for continued peace, were nil. The probabilities posed in the *Theory of Business Enterprise* were now all but settled, in favor of movement toward an increasingly totalitarian society dominated by businessmen, but allowing onto the stage of power those imbued with the military outlook. And once that process began, the businessman himself would find himself pushed to the side. The mind of man, like the products he consumed, and the jobs he worked, would become standardized. Like his Roman ancestors, he would achieve some modicum of material well-being, at a price: *"Panem et circenses*: The Bread Line and the Movies"* (XI, 453).

America, rather than being an industrial democracy bent on peace, declared Veblen, would find itself increasingly embroiled in the international politics of the European powers, and increasingly bent on following in their footsteps.

And in due proportion as the nation's statecraft is increasingly devoted to the gainful pursuit of international intrigue it will necessarily take on a more furtive character, and will conduct a larger proportion of its ordinary work by night and cloud. Which leads to a substitution of coercion in the place of consultation in the dealings of the official personnel with their underlying population, whether in domestic or foreign policy; and such coercion is increasingly accepted in a complaisant, if not a grateful, spirit by the underlying population, on a growing conviction that the national integrity is best provided for by night and cloud. So therefore it also follows that any overt expression of doubt as to the national expediency of any obscure transaction or line of transactions entered into by the official personnel in the course of this clandestine traffic in gainful politics, whether at home or abroad, will presumptively be seditious . . . (X, 444).

Appendix to Chapter 4

Veblen did not foresee everything, of course; nor, given his own view as to how social analysis develops, could he. Of the many major developments of this century, however, there are two that today are of such importance that it seems appropriate to comment on Veblen's neglect of them. One, the breakdown of colonialism, Veblen slighted completely; the second, the present position and meaning of the Soviet Union, he approached only in an oblique fashion. In what follows, we shall not attempt to make excuses for Veblen, but will attempt to explain why the present importance of these matters escaped him.

Except for two unimportant essays, Veblen ceased to write after 1923, more from the weariness that issues from despair than from old age. Although there are infrequent references to colonialism in Veblen's writings, and one essay (in XI, 361-82) directly dealing with colonies, he did not anticipate the political and economic turbulence in these areas so characteristic of recent years.* The question of imperialism was much bruited about in the years before World War I; but the apparent strength of the competing metropolitan powers precluded speculation on the disintegration of their empires. Attention was rather on the attendant conflicts among the Great Powers. When colonial disintegration began, it was the product of a many-sided process made up of worldwide depression, the growth of Soviet power and prestige, the unsettling and weakening effects of two world wars, and, associated with all these, the spread simultaneously of hope and unrest in the colonial areas. Veblen's last decade of productivity was one that began with the rumblings of World War I and ended, as Veblen saw it, with the sure vision that the Armistice was but a breathing space between World War I, the spread of barbarism, and the resumption of even more devastating and encompassing warfare. Given such a terrifying prospect, it is not surprising that Veblen failed to foresee the rise of the poor countries to independence and well-being a happy condition whose likelihood is still at best unclear.

Interestingly enough, Veblen's view of the ephemerality of economic leadership, and of the rapidity by which backward areas can catch up by the adoption of technologies in fresh institutional situations, did allow him to make one comment of current interest:

America has been a land of unexampled natural resources. Some day China and the Russian dominions will presumably outbid America in that way, both as to the abundance and the availability of their natural re-

---

* Nor, in his time, did anyone else. However, there is much of value in Veblen for understanding and guiding the process of development in the underdeveloped countries.

sources, and Brazil and Argentina come into the same class in this respect, as also other less well known regions in the low latitudes. . . . As the case stands just now these regions are outlying tributaries to the industrial system that centers in the north-temperate latitudes, and they come into the industrial scheme as a necessary compliment [*sic*] to the ways and means of this industrial system rather than a basis for self-balanced industrial commonwealths at home. All of that may be due to change presently (X, 166).

Veblen wrote several articles directly or obliquely concerned with the Russian Revolution (see XI). Apart from a casually sympathetic attitude toward the aims of the revolution, Veblen's attention was held by the role of the Soviet Union in the calculations of the Great Powers. Veblen took for granted that the capitalist economies of the West would do all in their power to destroy the revolution and to prevent the "infection" from spreading (XI, 404). In a savage review of Keynes's *Economic Consequences of the Peace*, Veblen argued that the essence of the Treaty of Versailles

is an unrecorded clause by which the governments of the Great Powers are banded together for the suppression of Soviet Russia. . . . Apart from this unacknowledged compact there appears to be nothing in the Treaty that has any character of stability or binding force. Of course, this compact for the reduction of Soviet Russia was not written into the text of the Treaty; it may rather be said to have been the parchment upon which the text was written (XI, 464).

Veblen thought the idea of Soviet Russia as a *military* menace to the Western powers was patently absurd, given its low level of economic development and postwar impoverishment; but it was this same backwardness he saw as Russia's main strength in holding off the Allied military intervention in Russia in the years immediately following the war:

[114]

. . . the Soviet owes this measure of success to the fact that the Russian people have not yet been industrialized in anything like the same degree as their western neighbors. They have in great measure been able to fall back on an earlier, simpler, less close-knit plan of productive industry; such that any detailed part of this loose-knit Russian community is able, at a pinch, to draw its own livelihood from its own soil by its own work, without that instant and unremitting dependence on materials and wrought goods drawn from foreign ports and distant regions, that is characteristic of the advanced industrial peoples (IX, 95).

Veblen recognized a menace of another type stemming from Russian Bolshevism (i.e., Communism). In a long article entitled "Bolshevism Is a Menace—to Whom?" Veblen answered his own question by replying:

Bolshevism is revolutionary. It aims to carry democracy and majority rule over into the domain of industry. Therefore it is a menace to the established order and to those persons whose fortunes are bound up with the established order (XI, 400).

The list of those "menaced" directly for Veblen was a list of the "vested interests of western Christendom." And if the common man is devoid of a share in these vested interests, does he then have reason to welcome the Bolshevik revolution, and the "infection" spreading from it, with open arms? It might seem so; but

. . . such a hasty view overlooks the great lesson of history that, when anything goes askew in the national economy, or anything is to be set to rights, the common man eventually pays the cost and he pays it eventually in lost labor, anxiety, privation, blood, and wounds. The Bolshevik is the common man who has faced the question: What do I stand to lose? and has come away with the answer: Nothing. And the elder statesmen are busy with arrangements for disappointing that indifferent hope (XI, 414).

Because of his preoccupation with this consequence of the Russian Revolution and his implicit expectation that the "elder statesmen" of the West would somehow succeed in sidetracking the revolution, Veblen did not venture a serious analysis of the prospects of the Soviet system. However, his view of the process of economic and social change closely fits the history of the Soviet Union in the past forty years or so, as regards 1) the difficulties and the harshness of its development, and, seemingly in conflict, 2) the speed of industrial development and the recent softening of Soviet controlling institutions.

At the time of the revolution, Russia was among the most "backward" of European nations in its social institutions and its level of economic development. In Veblen's genetic analysis, the speed with which a revolutionary group could change society would be inversely proportional to the degree of difference between what it attempted and what it had to work with. What the Soviet bureaucracy inherited from the Czars was an autocratic and repressive political system, an illiterate, poor, and predominantly rural population, a few islands of modern industry (largely foreign-owned and controlled up to 1917), badly located natural resources and poor systems of transportation, communications, and power, the leavings of war and civil war, and a hostile world. Consequently, for Veblen, political dictatorship would have seemed the natural "next step," particularly given the ambitious economic aims of the Russian leaders. Although the enormous *problems* of economic development in the Soviet Union have not occasioned surprise to most outsiders, its substantial industrial *achievement* has. Both would fit into a Veblenian framework: the difficulties because of the initial backwardness and associated characteristics, the achievements because of "the advantage of coming late."

By this latter notion, developed by him with particular reference to German industrialization, Veblen referred to the ability of a society starting "afresh" to borrow the most promising technological and institutional features of older societies, and to adapt them free of the outworn "institutional furniture" on which they rested in the lands of their origin. This approach to technology does not refer solely to the latest in engineering developments. In the Soviet Union, its primary applicability lay in the ability of the Soviets to view modern technology as it must be viewed if it is to be used most efficiently: as a "comprehensive, close-knit, interlocking whole." This conception involves planning, and social control, and of course these constitute the essence of the Soviet economic system. The Russians borrowed the notion of planning from German developments surrounding World War I, used by them to enhance war production. The Russians took this approach to technology, joined it to state ownership and long-range planning for the entire economy, and it became a different scheme.

Whatever may be said of the enormous social and economic problems accompanying Soviet development, their industrial sector has been brought to a level of modernization and great strength. As Veblen viewed matters, the problems would be attributed to the attempt of the Soviets to go against the grain of tradition with an inadequate resource base; the achievement would also be attributed to their going against the grain of tradition, but with the help of borrowed technologies.

Chapter 5

THE STRENGTHS AND
WEAKNESSES OF VEBLEN

Thorstein Veblen presumed to be neither judge nor prophet, despite his many judgments and prophecies. Notwithstanding his view of himself, Veblen's readers seldom fail to be impressed by the telling ring of his judgments, the deadly accuracy of his expectations, the degree to which he caught the quality of the twentieth century.

We naturally admire those who see through their present to the future; but we measure the worth of a social scientist by something more enduring than his vision; and this leads us to ask several questions of Veblen. Did he develop procedures, hypotheses, theories, which can be used by others? Did he furnish an analytical framework adequate to the problems he tackled? Was his vision dependent upon scattered insights, or was it a product of a theoretical framework that can be used, and improved upon, by others with similar, or even different, values? When he was right, was he right for good reasons?*

It is not possible here—perhaps not at all—to give a definitive answer to these questions for Veblen. His work traversed a vast array of issues and problems, and his procedures were often left obscure. But before we go on to evaluate the usefulness of Veblen for contemporary social science let us first digress to examine the important question of "similar values."

---

* As will be touched upon below, a sharp line cannot be drawn between "hunch," insight, hypothesis, and theory. A "hunch" that leads to a systematic insight, taken together with experience and training, furnishes the basis for a hypothesis which, if validated, can become part of a theory, part of a *system* of explanation.

Veblen well understood the close relationship between the preconceptions and values of social scientists and the theories they construct. But, as noted earlier, Veblen regularly denied any involvement in the issues *he* analyzed. It was his style, after a trenchant criticism, to assert that he was *not* criticizing, which would have implied evaluation; that he was merely describing the "facts"—e.g., when, in the course of a devastating critique of American college education, he says, "it is by no means here assumed that learning is substantially more to be desired than proficiency in genteel dissipation" (VI, 89). If Veblen deluded others with this device, he surely did not fool himself. He often stated, for example, that "the reason for a denial"—such as the one above—"is the need for it" (e.g., IV, 258n). Veblen's style was a persistent, consummate irony. We must deduce the values of Veblen not from what he said of them, but from what he praised and attacked; we must ignore his disclaimers.

Veblen despised war, hypocrisy, waste, tyranny, conformity, patriotism, supernaturalism, privilege—"force and fraud." For him, the good society would be at once democratic, peaceable, efficient, just, and scientific. Such a society he described by the term "industrial democracy," and he placed emphasis on both the adjective and the noun. He believed that industrial democracy could emerge only if the institutions supporting and resting upon patriotism, religion, and money-making receded and disappeared. This was asking a lot, and because that is so there are not many who fully share Veblen's values. Veblen would say that our notions of what is good and right are derived from the institutions within which we have lived. Since we have all lived in large part within those institutions that Veblen looked upon as obstacles to human progress, few of us can survive Veblen's slashing critiques without at least an occasional sense of outrage.

But there are some. And there are others who, reading Veblen, "take thought," or have second thoughts, on matters they have taken for granted, matters challenged so incisively by Veblen. In this respect, Veblen has value apart from the theories he built, or apart from those he made possible. That value inheres in his exposure of the pervasiveness, the meaning, and the danger of the violent and the irrational in the world about us. It inheres in Veblen's delineation and explanation of what constitutes irrational behavior. In short, Veblen is useful for the process of *unlearning*, always an integral part of the process of learning.

Veblen never actively espoused the things he believed in, as we have seen. It was his life's work to attack those institutions* he saw as menacing to a healthy society. It was his assumption that the removal of "imbecile institutions" would allow the emergence of an industrial democracy. This happy development would signify and result from the triumph of the constructive instincts of man—the parental bent and the instincts of workmanship and idle curiosity. Had Veblen *expected* these developments—and he did not—he, no less than those he criticized, could be accused of being "teleological" in his analysis. But what Veblen thought desirable, he seldom expected to occur. Not expecting any substantial improvement in the condition of man—indeed, despairing of it—Veblen constructed no program of reform or action to bring it about. Like Marx, he did not "concoct kitchen recipes for the future."** Marx did not do so (except in general statements concerning socialism) because he appreciated the difficulties of institutional prescriptions for a future situation that could be dimly apprehended at best. But Marx, if with excessive optimism, did specify the process by which change could (and, he thought, would) be brought about, and Marx participated in the political process moving along those lines. It may be offered that Marx's optimism was one factor leading him to take pains in systematizing his theory.

Veblen's gloomier position, apart from any more personal

---

* One noted critic of Veblen, whom politeness suggests be left nameless, has claimed that Veblen was "against institutions." This absurd idea, if it means anything, is tantamount to saying that a doctor who prescribes preventive medical care, or who advises surgery, is "against bodies."

** The widespread belief that Veblen did so, in his "Memorandum on a Practicable Soviet of Technicians" (IX, 138 ff.), will be examined in later pages.

factors, led him to neglect serious discussion of the process by which desirable change might be brought about. But Veblen was gloomy not only in his social analysis. Pessimism pervaded his entire existence, coloring his marriages, his career, and his daily associations. Veblen was a recluse who, if he found satisfaction in attacking society and its stuffed shirts, found joy only "outside" society: he loved animals, he loved making things with his hands, he loved books. His writings reveal this quality of the recluse, of the outsider; and this quality gave to Veblen's works their chief merit as well as their chief defect. This point will bear more detailed examination.

Veblen was a teacher of economics for much of his life. His teaching had at least two qualities in common with his writings: 1) he was a source of life-long inspiration for a small group of devoted students; 2) he was virtually unintelligible, at times even inaudible, in the classroom. When Veblen taught, he mumbled, and in a low voice. It may be said of his writings that they, too, often "mumble, and in a low voice."

Veblen's performance as a teacher and writer was integrally connected to his general outlook. That outlook informed him that it is not only virtually hopeless to seek progressive change; it is also personally foolhardy. Veblen may have been correct to some degree in both these assumptions; but he acted on them at times in an extreme, self-defeating, manner.* His professional career was unavoidably turbulent, given his unconventional ideas and his unconventional personal life. But a reading of Veblen's life reveals some moments, at least, when he effectually encouraged an unsatisfactory situation to persist or to develop; instances occur, as a sociologist might put it, of "the self-fulfilling prophecy."

---

* For example, on the personal level, in 1925 Veblen was in effect offered the presidency of the American Economic Association (of which he was not a member), the highest honor that can be accorded to an economist. He turned the offer down, essentially out of bitterness. (Interestingly enough, the move to gain this office for Veblen was begun by Professor Paul Douglas, later to be Senator from Illinois.)

Veblen's personal life is revealing, but of greater importance here are his writings. Taken together, they illuminate contradictions which Veblen never resolved, and which weakened his contribution to understanding. On the one hand, Veblen is one of the wordiest and most repetitive of writers. His meaning is frequently unclear; his sentences are often long, rambling, involute; he is often vague to the point of cloudiness. Also, as we have seen, he presumed himself to be aloof from the social maelstrom. On the other hand, Veblen was witty. He could with a succinct phrase rip away what had been in others' hands a tangled mat of confusion. When he was clear, his words snapped and sparkled. And his writings are almost entirely occupied with the origins, the nature, and the meaning of the social problems concerning which he pretended insouciance.

In the face of these considerations, one may presume that when Veblen was unclear, he had allowed himself—or had chosen—to be. Social indifference does not easily square with the prodigious effort supporting Veblen's analyses of social issues. One need not be psychiatrically inclined to infer that Veblen's protestations of indifference were a form of camouflage. But camouflage that can confuse one's enemies can to the same degree confuse one's friends. Unfortunately, Veblen probably confused his followers more than those he despised, if only because the former were the more likely to read him.

Veblen was against waste, but his own writings were generally as inefficient as the business system he attacked. He was merciless in his analyses of "devout observances" and "ceremonial ritual," but he played these games himself; even though he did so ironically, the result was that he "threw sand in his own gears." To all this, Veblen might respond that the possibilities for social improvement, and for finding a serious and influential audience, were so dim as to make care and seriousness inappropriate. However, it is difficult to believe that Veblen's impressive contributions were made without some hope that his efforts might have meaning. That they did have meaning is indicated by the economists and sociologists (among others) who have acknowledged their indebtedness to Veblen, and by the even greater number of those who have unknowingly been influenced by him. That his camouflage and lack of clarity worked against his own purposes, on the other hand, is indicated by the feckless works of some of those who have attempted to follow his leads.

The preceding interpretation raises the suspicion that much of what is obscure in Veblen was calculated to be so. Much else seemingly reflects a casual attitude toward important questions, as a result of Veblen's deeply if not consistently held conviction that there was nothing much that could be done; even, as David Riesman has argued, that "nobody was listening."

Veblen's contribution towers above that of any other American economist, however much he has left to be done, and however difficult it is to work with what he left us. It is saying a great deal of Veblen to point out that the structure he built is strongest in its foundations and weakest in its superstructure. For those who share his values, those foundations provide a substantial and enduring base on which to build. But, as with other great economists, such as Keynes and Marx, one need not *fully* share Veblen's values to find his approach useful. This is true to the degree that Veblen illuminated particular strategic relationships in the functioning of society. One need not find Veblen congenial to find him helpful.

Having digressed to assess the sources of Veblen's weaknesses, let us now attempt to distinguish between the solid and the insubstantial in his writings, appreciating at the outset that in Veblen's work his strengths and his weaknesses intermingle in a complex, often inextricable manner. Veblen's method is the appropriate starting point for such an appraisal; it is there we are most likely to find an answer to the questions posed earlier: in brief, "when Veblen was right, was he right for good reasons?" Veblen was "right" about so much, in his own day, and down to the present, that it seems implausible to credit "luck" as the explanation.*

---

* It is seemingly less implausible to argue that, because Veblen's predictions were almost all on the gloomy side, and the world is a

Veblen's approach may be seen as having two major components: 1) his emphasis on genetic analysis—i.e., his concern with the origins, the present functioning, and the future probabilities associated with a given situation; 2) his assumptions and key variables. These two aspects of Veblen's approach were not separated, of course; but in general it may be said that Veblen's superiority to the neo-classical economists—for those currently interested in economic processes and problems—is primarily due to the first of these; the greater accuracy of Veblen's predictions over those of Marx results from his asumptions and key variables. In pursuing these points in more detail, one should also indicate the areas in which the objects of Veblen's criticisms of economics had strengths he lacked.

It is generally agreed that neo-classical economics is "welfare economics." The concern of the value and distribution theories that comprise this school of economics is the question: "What are the principles of optimal choice?" Or, more specifically, "under assumed institutional and technological conditions, and irrespective of time and place, what will maximize welfare?"* This is another way of stating the ques-

---

vale of tears, he was bound to be "right" more often than not. Apart from the fact this is in itself a "theory" of sorts, the contention may be answered by pointing out that Veblen was not merely gloomy; he specified the *manner* in which relevant processes would work out, with what he would call "a cause and effect, genetic analysis." That Veblen also left unexamined much that is important for understanding the problems he deemed vital will be taken up subsequently.

* It is this aspect of such economics that has led it to be called "Robinson Crusoe economics": that is, an economics that is as meaningful in the simple setting of a desert island as in modern England —or as meaningless. It must be pointed out that neo-classical economics is not as "institutionally neutral" as our characterization may suggest, or as some of its adherents would believe. It assumes private property in the means of production, takes a profit-maximizing businessman as its decision-making focus, assumes away market restraints from either the business or the labor side, and posits the absence of social intervention. It frequently concludes by opposing the real development of the constraints assumed away in the model. Thus, "laissez-faire" economics. The few "pure" adherents of this school today oppose any and all departures from the free and unfettered operation of markets for all goods and services—to an extent that goes so far as to decry public education. It is fair to say that such an economics does more to attract its adherents than

tion: "Assuming no institutional constraints, what constitutes completely 'rational' behavior?" Here "rational" means that the *sole* problem is one of making the most of scarce resources, and that the actors are motivated only by rational considerations.

The criticisms of the neo-classical approach made by Veblen and other institutionalists have not caused the neo-classicists to abandon their assumptions and theories; but such criticisms have influenced some neo-classicists to make their assumptions more explicit, to become more conscious of the limitations of their analyses, and (for all but the "purists") to abandon earlier pretenses that the world they discuss in fact exists. Consequently, if some of Veblen's criticisms no longer ring true, a major reason is that his arguments had a reforming effect on economics.

In earlier pages the assumptions of neo-classical economics were subjected to Veblen's critique; here several things will be said of the analysis from a contemporary standpoint. By assumption and by focus, the neo-classical economist is led to ignore 1) the persistent clash of interests in society, as reflected in the realm of politics and social movements, and 2) the fundamental and unsettling force of technology and technological change. In taking institutions as given, the neo-classical economist 3) is led to define as an improvement in welfare only those changes that involve neither social conflict nor institutional change, and 4) is inhibited from examining the social process at all, except as something "outside" the theory.*

In these and other respects, such an economics, whatever else it may achieve, serves to deflect attention from social relationships and processes that tend to upset the status quo.

---

it does to produce them. It also has a hand in turning many away from economics.

* The practical meaning of the neo-classical approach is underlined when it is recognized that "welfare economics" not only provides no guidelines for those involved or interested in constructing "the welfare state," it is a body of theory that—given its assumptions—stands in opposition to any such developments. To one degree or another, "welfare" developments are taking place; but they are taking place with little or no *theoretical* basis in economics.

Such analysis does not tend to *maintain* the status quo, for that *cannot* be maintained. But it does absorb energies in the pursuit of universal principles of rational economic conduct—energies that might, with different training, be spent in attempting to understand how the ever-changing "status quo" can be led to change in ways more beneficial than detrimental to mankind. It should be clear that theory concerned directly with the factors making for change in society can serve conservative, liberal, or radical ideologies—of course, in different measure and with different emphases. But when the social process is abstracted from by economists to the point where only those on the fringes of the discipline are concerned with the problems of change, all of society is the worse for it.*

The material welfare of society is determined most importantly by changes taking place over time; consequently, the focus of the neo-classical economist on the "short-run" (defined so as to preclude both technological and institutional change) renders him incapable of examining the very question he takes up and that society expects him to take up. It may be argued with some justice that it is not the economist's function to seek answers to questions predicated by laymen. With equal justice it may be asked, If the economist does not occupy himself with the moving economic questions of his day—even if that leads him into the muddy fields where economic, social, and political institutions are stirred by technological change and human aspirations—who will? We need not search long or far for an answer. The economist alone has the professional function to examine and understand the economic interests of society as a whole; when he abdicates that function, whether by conscious choice or by the focus and method of his analysis, he leaves the public unarmed to face the continuing and self-seeking thrusts of "the vested interests"—in business, in labor, in agriculture, in politics, or wherever they may exist.

Neo-classical economics, whether in the past or the pres-

* Unless, of course, one holds to the view that the scientific analysis of society is neither possible nor desirable nor necessary. But that view is seldom taken today; least of all by social scientists.

ent, *has* contributed to our understanding of certain basic, "purely economic," questions. These are questions of enduring interest—irrespective of time, place, ideology, or technology. They are questions that revolve around the problem of scarce resources and rational choice between competing uses of such resources—a problem for societies institutionally and technologically so diverse as eighteenth century England, nineteenth century America, and twentieth century China. The analysis of such problems legitimately and necessarily entails a high level of abstraction. Veblen rejected such analysis peremptorily, perhaps too much so. If they are to be approached wisely, even in the "affluent society" of the United States, there are problems of choice that require the kind of "rational" economics developed in neo-classical theory.

The question, therefore, is not whether neo-classical economics has *any* usefulness or meaning; it surely has some.* The more serious question is concerned with balance. Is the training, the time, the energy, the output of economists devoted to refining neo-classical analysis proportionate to the range of economic problems confronting society? The question is not, should the principles of rational choice be clarified? Of course they should. But, with so much else demanding clarification by economists, it would appear that Veblen's out-of-hand rejection of this economics comes closer to a correct judgment of how economists should use their skills—and what skills they should develop—than does the present bias of the discipline. This position is given added weight when it is understood that all too frequently the neo-classical analysis is applied to problems to which it is wildly inappropriate—problems centering on change and institu-

---

* Paradoxically, it is probably correct to say that the economics of choice developed by the bourgeois economists of western capitalist societies has much greater usefulness in planned socialist economies than in the economies for which it was developed. If this is so, it is because the matters taken as "given" in neo-classical economics are under much more, if not by any means complete, control in socialist than in capitalist economies; also, there is presently a greater "scarcity problem" in, say, the Soviet Union than in, say, the United States. (The same comment would be true of mathematical economics and econometrics.)

tional conflict—by economists whose narrow training prevents them from recognizing the relevant "institutional variables" —the relevant "facts."*

This question may be put differently. Of what value are the principles of rational choice when the institutions of society prevent rational choices from being made? Of what use is an economics concerned with scarcity when society finds itself plagued by its inability to utilize already existing resources—natural, human, and man-made? The answer is not, "of no use." Celestial navigation, for example, may be a useful art even to those on a sinking ship; perhaps, even, on a cloudy night. But other kinds of knowledge are at such times considerably more important. These other kinds of knowledge (e.g., what it is that prevents rational choices from being made) Veblen emphasized; although in attempting to redress the balance, he may have swung back too far.

In contrast to the neo-classical economists—and many conventional economists still today—Veblen took as the central problem of the economist 1) the restlessness and imperatives of technology, 2) the institutions shaping human behavior, 3) the social psychology of man, and 4) the interaction of all these as determining the quality of a society at any time and as giving rise to social change and conflict.

Veblen said of the neo-classicists that "their arguments have been as good as the premises on which they proceed" (VII, 86). Veblen's own arguments—concerning the structure and functioning of the economy, and related social and political processes—have been largely validated by subsequent events, and we may credit his "premises" as the explanation. The choice of premises, or assumptions, is a matter of judgment; it is a resultant of some combination of values, knowledge, and insight. In the mind of a careful thinker, such

* The excessive degree to which refinements of neo-classicism have been carried is suggested by a highly placed and highly trained theoretical economist now in government circles who has remarked that all that is useful in neo-classical theory in his own work (which involves, among other things, the allocation of scarce resources to competing ends) is taught on the sophomore level in college economic courses. See *Business Week*, January 5, 1963, p. 19.

judgments become hypotheses, the validity of which is tested against events. The economist assumes that "events"—i.e., the real world—are the matters directly concerning the theorist. Unlike the neo-classical economists, Veblen saw the real world as the only legitimate concern of the economist; anything else amounted to exercises in logic, or versions of what he called "homiletical exegesis."

The kind of world Veblen saw about him was one in which efforts to develop a refined calculus of choice were a form of conspicuous waste at best; a dangerous luxury, at worst. The world's problem was to prevent retrogression into barbarism. The many dimensions of that problem require for its understanding the greatest diligence, the greatest co-operation, the greatest good sense that social scientists can muster. For Veblen, the world was not steadily climbing a mountain at whose peak it would find Utopia; it was a world constantly poised on the edge of a frightful abyss. If it was not to fall into that abyss, it must move away from it; and that, even for Veblen, meant climbing the happy mountain. But Veblen was more concerned with the abyss than with the mountain. He was a pessimist; not least because he thought that man could be led to confuse abyss with mountain; to accept, even to cherish, a social process that meant deprivation of spirit, of material comfort, and of life itself. Whether Veblen's theory made him a pessimist, or his pessimism shaped his theory, and how these may have interacted, is an interesting question, but not a vital one. We should be interested in the validity and usefulness of theory rather more than with its psychiatric origins.

Adequate social theory is not of course a sufficient condition for preventing social disaster or for bringing about social improvement. Theory must be matched with action. But adequate theory is necessary if social action is to be sufficient. Without understanding the process of social change, socially active groups will move only by chance and good fortune in persistently and enduringly beneficial directions. History is strewn with the wreckage left by well-motivated individuals and groups, shattered by forces they did not comprehend and could not control.

We do not possess an adequate theory of society or of social change. Marx, it may be said, attempted one. With all the limitations of Marxian theory, it has proved to be more influential than Veblenian theory. Among other reasons, Veblenian "theory" is so unsystematic; it is, in an important sense, implicit rather than explicit. It is also riddled with gaps and marred by unsupported, at times unsupportable, generalizations.

Veblen's contribution suffers both because of Veblen's personality and temperament, and because of factors outside and beyond him. Pessimism and caution interacted to deprive Veblen of both the morale and the courage required to develop a forthright, systematic body of theory. His rôle as a radical social critic, in addition, placed him at a disadvantage he could not overcome.

The radical social critic is fated to work at a disadvantage that affects his ability to develop a rounded body of adequately supported conclusions; for some, the will to make the effort is finally weakened. *Because* he is radical, the radical critic early finds himself concerned with an immense range of issues, however narrow his initial focus may have been. The study of leaves is complicated; but to trace the leaf to the twig, the twig to the branch, the branch to the trunk, and the trunk to its roots and the soil in which it grows; and to understand each aspect and the processes and relationships tying each to the other is much more difficult. To drop the metaphor, to attempt this for society is an infinitely more complex study of another and much greater magnitude. It was this latter study that Veblen attempted. The analytical and empirical challenges involved in such an enormous task are themselves forbidding; to attempt them single-handedly is impossible.

Like other radicals before and since his time, Veblen found himself working almost alone. In the nature of things, and for reasons Veblen himself described, the unconventional analyst is bound to be surrounded by those who accept things as they are. Veblen lived in a society that seemed almost eager to accord with his gloomiest observations. He associated with colleagues who viewed him with some com-

bination of tolerant amusement, hostility, and almost determined obliviousness to the facts of life and the imperatives
of social theory. It is little wonder that his theory was less
than completely worked out. It is little wonder, too, that as
the years passed, Veblen became increasingly intemperate,
and even shrill, in his judgments. Veblen was scarcely a
genial observer of the social scene as a young man; he
began as a bemused skeptic. But he ended his life in bitterness—secluded, alone, a virtual anchorite.

In the nature of things, one may suppose, a critic such
as Veblen will be judged by his defects more than by his
virtues, if only because a full recognition of such virtues
might produce discomfort in the judges. Veblen's defects are
undeniable. Some of these have been suggested earlier;
more will be touched on now, although there will be no
attempt to reproduce them in full catalogue. It will be useful
to indicate the weaknesses in Veblen's areas of greatest
strength, for here the most fruitful use may be made of his
work. Thus it will appear that the few moments of optimism
in Veblen were no more and no less justified than the
pervasive optimism of Karl Marx; it will appear, also, that
society is even more complicated than Veblen proposed. If
some of these complications add to the problems that Veblen saw, others may provide a basis for hopeful developments that he overlooked. Thus a brief re-examination of 1)
Veblen's theories of the leisure class and conspicuous consumption, 2) his theory of instincts, 3) his distinction between "business" and "industry," and 4) his treatment of
nationalism will indicate the manner in which Veblen's
ideas may still be put to use. For the sake of convenience,
these four aspects of his thought will be intermingled in the
following discussion.

Veblen's *Theory of the Leisure Class* made its mark as a
witty, skeptical view of the foibles of mankind, but it is
more importantly the foundation for a theory of power and
prestige. It is generally accepted that a theory of social
change must include a theory of the state—i.e., an explanation of the sources and uses of power. In Marx, the theory
of the state rests upon his concept of "the ruling class,"

whose power derives from the ownership and control of the means of production. Given the ruling class, and the opposed interests of the working class, social change centers on the class struggle motivated by clashing economic interests.

The closest thing to a ruling class in Veblen is "the vested interests." Veblen's theory of the leisure class provides an explanation of how and why the vested interests gain, hold, and use power; and, through his concept of "emulation," Veblen shows how and why the "common man" seeks to be like, rather than to overthrow, the vested interests. The root of Veblen's difference with Marx lies in Veblen's having added "prestige" to "power." This is to say that Veblen integrated social psychology—if inadequately—with the economics and politics analyzed by Marx.*

Power in America, for Veblen, is gained and held through the ownership and control of wealth (whereas in Veblen's Germany, increasing economic power combined with traditional military and political strength). State power is the expression of the interests of dominant business groups. Politics is the manifestation of this relationship. Should military power grow, it is at the behest, or with the acquiescence, of business rulers. The latter comprise but a tiny percentage of the total population. They wield authority without overt coercion and without challenge because of supportive social institutions and the emulative propensities of the underlying population. These propensities have two major outlets: patriotism and conspicuous consumption. In turn, patriotism and conspicuous consumption (and patterns of behavior related to them) are maintained and encouraged 1) by the steady support given to the aims and values and interests of the "vested interests" by the institutional frame-

* The late C. Wright Mills, in his *Power Elite* (1956) and other writings, combined Veblen and Marx (and others) in his own analysis, which he developed a generation after Veblen's death. Mills's "elite" is composed of three basic groups—business, political, and military—which interact in a manner compatible with, but more complicated than, that posited by Veblen. The degree of additional complication revolves around the problems and possibilities posed by contemporary technology, taken in the context of the Cold War.

work of a business enterprise society—not least by its educational system, the media of communication, and the courts —and 2) by the predatory instincts of man. The process of social change resulting from these relationships is compounded of economic inefficiency and waste, a *de facto* political oligarchy, and intermittent warfare, the last acting as a solvent of economic depression and social unrest. Working against this unhappy process, but without substantial effect, are the constructive instincts of man: the parental bent, the instinct of workmanship, and the instinct of idle curiosity.*

In its main outlines, Veblen's theory of the state, which rests upon the nature, functioning, and maintenance of the "vested interests," appears to have considerable validity. Businessmen and business values dominate the thinking of most Americans, so much so that they are accepted "unthinkingly." There are, however, divisions of opinion within the business community. Even more to the point, there are divisions of opinion between business groups as a whole and those whom Veblen would take as their kept creatures—in government, in organized religion, in labor, in the schools and universities, and in the media of communication; there is conflict between the values and pressures of business society and the broader values Americans (including some businessmen) choose to think they hold. These broader values are quite compatible with Veblen's expectations concerning the "constructive instincts," but they go beyond the implications of that concept.

As the entire world shivers with the fear of a thermonuclear war and seems unable to come to grips with it, it would not be seemly to make too much of the cracks in the solid front of what Veblen called "predators"; but that nuclear war has been skirted for this long suggests that considerations other than those dealt with by Veblen may have intruded for a while. Veblen contended that the longer that "while" could be extended, the greater the reasons for expecting beneficial social change. Whether we agree or dis-

---

* No attempt can be made here to view Veblen's instinct theories against contemporary psychological theories; it is clear that such an attempt would find many areas both of congruence and of conflict.

agree with Veblen, it becomes necessary to explore the nature of, reasons for, and means of enhancing existing complexities in "the structure of social forces."

The world has changed swiftly and dramatically since Veblen died. If much of that change has been disastrous, and much of it along the lines he expected, some of it contains hopeful possibilities. In recent years the American people have participated in a process of mounting xenophobia which is more substantial, more pervasive, and more lasting than that dissected by Veblen in his "Dementia Praecox" in 1922, when he wrote that "a Practicable Power has to rest its case on a nerve-shattering popular fear of aggression from without" (XI, 424). The conformity and patriotism marking the present, embedded in and supporting the Cold War, come uncomfortably close to the kind of thing envisaged by Veblen in the last pages of *The Theory of Business Enterprise*—down to and including the rapidly increasing influence of military criteria, and the manner in which the latter tend increasingly to take priority over "businesslike" criteria.

Both the technology of warfare and the rhetoric of the Cold War must be taken into consideration in assessing the long-run prospects for peace and war. Veblen, who dwelt so much on technology, recognized that technology had transformed warfare and diplomacy; but he did not and could not take account of a military technology that would, if used, annihilate both victor and vanquished. Whether or not the fear of mutual annihilation will cause the world's leaders to avoid nuclear war in the future cannot be more than guessed at; but that this element of the contemporary situation requires modification of Veblen's analysis may be stated firmly.

At present the hopes introduced by military technology are somewhat less commanding than the fears; but there is another, less obvious element, one which Veblen did not directly confront and which must also be considered.* It has to do with the rhetoric of national and international politics today. That rhetoric strongly emphasizes notions of

* A sense in which Veblen did confront the question now to be discussed will be examined in our concluding pages.

democracy and material well-being for all. Its economic manifestations emphasize consumer well-being and economic security. Whether and to what degree such rhetoric is honored in fact is of course important; but the rhetoric has an importance of its own, the more so the longer the world persists without war. Today, the major powers of the world —East and West—are under pressure to "produce," economically and politically, to a degree not approximated when Veblen wrote. It is easy to show that the most important product of these new factors is an endless "improvement" in the art of public relations, designed to create a "decorous" national appearance. Again, there is more to the matter than public relations; how much more is a matter for investigation. The astounding productivity of modern technology creates the possibility—and, it can be argued, the necessity —that rhetoric and reality, with appropriate pressure and direction, will move closer together than Veblen thought possible. On the other hand, we shall have missed what Veblen taught if we ignore the possibility that the rhetoric itself can continue to be altered to suit a garrison state society along the lines suggested in Orwell's *1984*. The tension between the hopeful and the dreadful possibilities constitutes the drama of this century.

An energetic, updated, systematic adaptation and use of Veblen's approach today would imply a substantial rehabilitation of the social sciences, as well as a cogent and clear-eyed appraisal of the nature of existing social problems. Problems of structure and ideology, cutting across disciplines, caught up in process, and centering upon the relationships between institutions and technology grip us today. They are problems that cannot be comprehended, let alone resolved, by analyses that take institutions as given and ignore the problems and possibilities posed by today's technology.

In the domestic realm, we need not speculate for long on the problems of most concern. They include persistent high-level unemployment, an inadequate rate of economic growth, a developing educational crisis, a spreading pall of conformity, urban blight, and a substantial and enlarging hard core of poverty—all this and more in the "affluent society." Internationally, we are confronted with the already great and growing strength of the Communist world, the "urge to industrialize" and widespread unrest in the underdeveloped areas, and the politics and economics of the European Common Market.

One need not be a Veblenian to recognize these problems or to see that, at home and abroad, they are significantly related to each other, both in their origin and in their potential resolution. But, even when the conventional social scientist possesses such recognition, he nonetheless allows a broad chasm to stand between what he appreciates and what, as a specialized professional, he studies. Specialization is of course necessary, in the social sciences as elsewhere, when specialization is the opposite of dilettantism. But specialization and trivialization are not the same thing.

Specialization in Veblen's time was just beginning to emerge in the social sciences; today it approaches the limits of credibility. More to the point, specializations are steadily separated from the main trunk of thought and problems of which they are presumed to be branches. Today, specialization—and its natural offspring, quantification—takes on a life of its own that increasingly makes technique competitive with perspective, rather than complementary. To the degree that unwitting specialization characterizes the social sciences, they accumulate more "knowledge" while simultaneously reducing their ability to use that knowledge to understand the nature of social problems.

Today's problems lend themselves appropriately to a Veblenian analytical framework. Emphasis must be placed on the nature, the functioning, and the interaction of social institutions, which are always in some degree anachronistic and anomalous. The degree to which institutions are "senile" or "imbecilic" today, it may be asserted, is critical. The institutions most commanding attention in this respect are those clustering around the system of business enterprise and the national state.

Institutions come into being—consciously or unconsciously —as the means by which men as individuals and in groups, conflicting and cooperating, for better or for worse, organize and control social behavior. Institutions may emerge from an unspoken consensus, as a matter of custom; they may be created in the process of conscious struggle, as was true, for example, of our Constitution. Institutions emerge in many ways that lie between the extremes of accepted custom and revolutionary change. However they may arise, institutions tend over time to become a part and an expression of an ideology, a set of beliefs and principles supporting a way of life. Paradoxically, when institutions function effectively, the setting in which they exist is changed. As time goes on, therefore, institutions necessarily serve functions at least in part different from those for which they were initially suited. As time goes on, also, institutions become shelters for vested interests which, attempting to make the most of what they have, attempt also to prevent institutional change, and do so with power, habit, and law behind them. All this activity is recognized widely—e.g., in concepts such as "the social lag," and in the continuous re-interpretation of the Constitution provided by the courts.

The institutions providing the foundation of American capitalism (and, as we shall see, modern nationalism) are no exception to the foregoing generalizations. The historical and legal foundations of our economic institutions developed in an era of expanding agriculture, spreading trade, and early industrialism. In fact and in law our economic institutions have changed much as we have become an industrial society; but we incline still to evaluate proposals for institutional change in a mood appropriate to that world long past. A striking symbol of this inclination is the legal fiction of the corporation as a "person"; no less striking, but of greater importance, is the pervasive belief that the spirit of business enterprise is the only proper approach to the problems of an advanced industrial society.

Unemployment, low growth rates, hard-core poverty, and related "social" problems of urban congestion and inadequate educational and health facilities are domestic problems which the system of American business enterprise is unable or unwilling to tackle directly. As Veblen was quoted as saying earlier, "it is a question of what businessmen may be expected to do for cultural growth on the motive of profits." It is not the function of businessmen to deal with national economic problems such as unemployment; nor would we wish them to deal with, say, health problems, on the basis of expected profits.

The easy answer that the market system *can* handle these matters is made doubtful by pointing out that it *hasn't*. Indeed, these problems have emerged from an economy dominated by a market system—and have emerged both despite and because of that dominance. The subtler suggestion that the market system has been hampered and interfered with by taxes, labor unions, regulation, and the whole apparatus of modern society may be answered by asking a question: Who will or can turn the clock back, how, and how far, and in doing so explain the origins of these "intrusive institutions" apart from the evolution of an industrial society? For in no highly developed industrial society do we find this "apparatus" missing in any important degree.

In recent decades, and particularly since the depression of the thirties, many explicit departures have been made from the institutions of a free private enterprise system. But it is important to note two characteristics of that process of change: 1) it has taken place in a piecemeal fashion, usually on the assumption that it was a reaction to aberrations or emergencies; 2) it has been apologetic in spirit and halting in application. These characteristics have been due in part to the hold of the past over men's minds, including even those pressing for change; in part they have resulted from the continuing power of "the vested interests" to hold back change.

Veblen's analysis of the nature and meaning of business enterprise stemmed from a deep aversion to both business principles and businessmen; he formed his ideas about business in the midst of its most buccaneering period, and the illustrations he used, e.g., in *The Theory of Business Enterprise,* are most frequently drawn from the spectacular revelations of governmental investigations of the time. Writing in such a period, when businessmen were on their worst behavior, and regarding businessmen with skepticism even when at their best, Veblen not surprisingly failed to give credit where credit was due and attributed some evil where it was not deserved.

The "credit" due belongs not to businessmen as such, but to the function of competition within a business-enterprise system. Veblen was doubtless correct in assuming that businessmen had a mortal fear of competition; but he was just as surely incorrect in assuming that competition served no beneficial function whatsoever, that it was a mere multiplication of money-seekers. Veblen acknowledged the benefits of competition for an earlier period, but he failed to give it credit for the period in which he wrote.

The foregoing defect is relevant to Veblen's critical distinction between "business" and "industry." The virtues of the American economy Veblen attributed to industrialism as such; the defects he attributed to the aims and techniques of the business community. It seems more accurate to think that there are *some* virtues arising out of business self-seeking, and *some* problems arising out of industrialism. Veblen was generally correct; but for purposes of formulating sensible and feasible policies, finer distinctions are required. These in turn require investigations going beyond anything Veblen accomplished or contemplated.

It is not difficult to find grounds for accepting Veblen's notions that business aims and methods are basic to the waste, inefficiency, and general foolishness of much of contemporary economic life. After all, businessmen have made most of the relevant decisions. But matters would be even less desirable if the process of competition in the market were abandoned where it exists—keeping in mind that market competition that cuts costs is considerably less pervasive than the "competition" that, while maintaining prices through collusion, acts through advertising expenditures and trivial product differentiation. Still, Veblen's now widely accepted contention that modern technology will not support a beneficially competitive market structure (because it will efficiently support only a few firms) except in the early phases of growth in an industry has considerable validity. This contention would not seem a novel idea to conventional economists today; however, their time might usefully be spent pondering the institutional and legal implications of this approach rather than in spinning out the niceties of a perfectly competitive market in long-run equilibrium.

If Veblen was eager to find fault with business, he was disinclined to do the same with industry. Industrialism has grown up in many different institutional patterns, as different as those characterizing Great Britain, the United States, Germany, Japan, and the Soviet Union. In no case has industrialism emerged in what might be thought of as its "pure" terms: namely, under the guidance of "engineering criteria." Nor, one may say firmly, could it ever, as Veblen well knew. There have always been some problems associated with industrialism that seem independent of the *type* of institutional framework. They are problems having to do with morale, discipline, quality, efficiency, with the organization of large-scale activities. Conceivably one could specify institutions to meet such problems with perfection; but on the whole such an approach would be no less "make-believe," to use Veblen's phrase, than the make-believe idealizations of private enterprise and neo-classical economics. This is not to say that such problems are insoluble. Nor does it mean that some situations are not worse than others. It is to say rather than Veblen did not take such problems into account, that he attributed all evils of industrial operation to business control, and that such problems *are* important.

But if it is clear that Veblen was sometimes careless, it is not at all clear that he was mistaken in his main proposition which states that the aims and methods of business enterprise become increasingly unsuited to the needs of a developing industrial society. The heart of this conception is the interdependence of the modern economy, caused by an industrial technology. If that is the heart, the circulatory system is the flow of goods and services that is increasingly subject to arteriosclerosis as the structure of production, and the institutions that guide its use become both unbalanced and inadequate.

Today's persisting unemployment, low growth rates, and

hard-core poverty are the outcome of some combination of a technology that requires rapidly decreasing amounts of labor per unit of output, a structure of production critically dependent upon the market for durable goods (including weapons), a long period of high levels of income and associated satiation of consumer wants for manufactures (given the distribution of income), a pattern of market controls that prevents both price and wage reductions, and, most generally, the fact that we *are* a highly developed industrial capitalist society.

America enjoyed its greatest buoyancy during periods of rapid institutional and/or technological change (in both product and technique); they were periods of innovation. The day will never come when innovations are exhausted; but the impact of any particular product or technique innovation today, given the fact that it is taking place in a "larger" economy, is less than the same development would have been at an earlier day. Moreover, the "innovations" most needed today are in areas traditionally kept at arm's length from the market: they are in the realm of *social*, not individual, needs, and for their implementation *institutional* innovation is required. Since our educational system is inadequate, our medical facilities costly and scarce, our cities congested and blighted, our transportation system verging on paralysis, there is much obviously to be done. Doubtless it would stimulate the entire economy, relieve unemployment, increase our rate of growth, and lessen poverty, if needed changes were made.

Economists are of course aware of these problems, but their *theoretical* apparatus does not meet them. Economic analysis, as such, focusses upon the immediate past, the present, and the immediate future. The changes in ("micro-" and "macro-") economics since Veblen wrote are modifications of the neo-classical framework. Modern economists typically view neo-classical economics with healthy skepticism; but that economics remains their starting-point, both in their training and in their analyses. An economics built on assumptions of given institutions and technology, and of perfect mobility of capital and labor, is not suited to problems emerging from and requiring institutional and technological change, and rigidities in capital and labor markets. It is as if modern astro-physicists were to work with Ptolemaic astronomy and Aristotelian physics, much modified. Such an approach would not only be cumbersome; its initial perspective would be crippling.

Conventional economists characteristically limit their recommendations in the realm of public policy to a narrow range: more competition, for "micro" problems; monetary and fiscal policies for "macro" problems. There are difficulties in implementing "more competition" in industries where such a policy is neither politically feasible nor economically workable; apart from that, however, competition within an *industry* does not relieve structural imbalance in the *economy*. Competition, whatever its virtues, does not cause excess productive capacity to flow to areas of inadequate productive capacity, not just because there are rigidities in the market system, but because the areas of shortage are areas of public need and do not appear in the marketplace.

Nor do monetary and fiscal policies, however important they may be for short-run problems, act to promote long-run economic growth. It is not that there is no effect; for the short-run and the long-run growth are of course interrelated. When structural problems exist—unused capacity in coal, in machinery, in automobiles, in steel; and increasing groups of technologically unemployed labor, and new entrants to the labor market who are unable to find jobs at all—they can be resolved only by structural change, and monetary and fiscal policies do not achieve structural change, at least not by design. "Not by design." That is perhaps the problem.

Economists are often pleased to see themselves as objective scientists, as highly trained thinkers dispassionately examining the implications of assorted economic relationships. Economists *should* be objective, but they *are* not dispassionate—although many assume that by taking basic institutions as given and conducting abstract analyses they have combined objectivity and neutrality. Veblen adopted a neutral pose; but the pose was a matter of words, not of focus. In his teaching and writing, unlike most other economists, Veblen examined, he did not take as given, "the principles of action which underlie the current, businesslike scheme of economic life . . ."; Veblen questioned "the existing law and order" (VIII, 239). To achieve desirable structural change in the economy requires just such a questioning process, and it requires achieving structural change by design.

If economists are to move in this direction, it is frequently argued, they must sacrifice objectivity. More to the point, they must sacrifice a spurious neutrality. A doctor does not sacrifice his objectivity when he recommends that his patient give up smoking, change his diet, or undergo an operation. The economist is more like a doctor than a physicist, as is often presumed. To remain objective an economist must make his procedures specific, regard the relevant evidence honestly, and specify his values. He need not, and he cannot, give up his values, as though he were apart from the society he analyzes. Whatever his political or social views, no economist accepts *all* economic institutions in existence. The question is not whether economists should evaluate institutions or seek change; the question is the *degree* of institutional change required, why, in what combinations, and how it can be achieved most satisfactorily. It involves values, theory, and fact; it is a question not likely to be treated adequately if its legitimacy is denied. Consciously or not, by proposal or by default, economists are "in the business" of accepting or rejecting particular institutions. The "business" will be done better when it is carried on by those who know what they are about.

The approach implied above, the approach pursued by Veblen, requires not only that economics shed much of its synthetic purity; it requires that economics more consciously relate itself to the other social sciences. Institutions are *social* phenomena, caught up in and affecting history. An increased emphasis upon institutions in economics implies an increased emphasis on politics, sociology, psychology, and history. Sociologists and historians are not interested in Veblen by accident; nor is it surprising that social scientists find Veblen too general. He could not succeed in the task he set himself. What Veblen could not do alone, cooperating social scientists may be able to do. The attempt has not yet been made.

The necessity for broadening the analytical framework of the economist is all the more obvious when we turn to international economic problems. Questions of nationalism then intrude; but in the underdeveloped areas it is also clear that economic institutions appropriate to industrialization cannot be "created" without substantial and pervasive change in the politics and the culture of such societies—and in their relationships with the already industrialized societies. Secondly, when we examine the probabilities associated with the European Common Market, it is clear that political and economic issues inextricably intertwine. Thirdly, one need merely mention the problems raised by the Communist Bloc, to indicate the necessity for an analysis that combines "economic" considerations with those of nationalism and ideology. If economists have done much fruitful work regarding these problems, most of it has been done outside the mainstream of conventional analysis. Veblen's approach, used consciously, could increase the fruitfulness of such work in the future.

Veblen found himself in closest agreement with the economists of his day in the area having to do with the protective tariff. Veblen was an unyielding supporter of "free trade." Even here, however, Veblen approached the question differently from his economist colleagues. The free-trade economists usually cast their arguments in terms of the universal gains to be had from an absence of barriers to trade and investment, and in abstraction from basic questions of institutional and technological change. Veblen focussed on the damage done by such barriers and on the reasons for their existence; his argument not only supported free trade, but advocated the disappearance of the nation state, and for reasons going well beyond the achievement of economic efficiency.

Veblen took it as axiomatic that protective tariffs lessen the free flow of goods in world trade, protect vested interests behind national borders, render production less efficient than it might be, and increase the hardships of the common man:

> . . . any protective tariff is an obstruction to industry and a means of impoverishment, just so far as it is effective. The arguments to the contrary invariably turn out to be the pettifogger's special pleading for some vested interest or for a warlike national policy, and these arguments convince only those persons who are able to believe that a part is greater than the whole. It also lies in the nature of protective tariffs that they always cost the nation disproportionately much more than they are worth to those vested interests which profit by them. In this respect they are like any other method of business-like sabotage (VII, 133-34).*

The elimination of any protection for domestic business interests as regards foreign trade, Veblen argued, should be matched by the elimination of any protection of investments made abroad:

> Commercial traffic and investment [should] be accounted a private venture, in pursuit of which the merchant or investor is acting on his own initiative, for his own ends, at his own risk; in which his compatriots share neither profit nor loss, and for the successful issue of which they assume no collective responsibility. What it comes to is that the community [should] no longer collectively promote or safeguard any private enterprise in pursuit of private gain beyond its own territorial bounds (XI, 376).

---

* To the common argument that "infant industries" need protection and that such protection benefits the entire society over the long run, Veblen, and most other economists, would reply that the same function can be provided by well-designed subsidies. It is politics, not economics, that supports the "infant-industry" case.

Going considerably further than the conventional econ-omist, Veblen saw the nation state as a tool of the business system (just as in other connections, he saw the industrial system as a tool of the militarists): ". . . so far as concerns their place and value in modern economic life, the national frontiers are a means of capitalistic sabotage . . ." (XI, 387).

More broadly, Veblen regarded the very existence of the nation state as a dangerous anachronism, on grounds of economics and of domestic and international politics. The nation state is incompatible with modern industry, with so-cial progress, and with peace. On the first score, he wrote:

> As an industrial unit, the nation is out of date. . . . Life and material well-being are bound up with the effectual working of the industrial system; and the industrial system is of an international character—or it should per-haps rather be said that it is of a cosmopolitan charac-ter, under an order of things in which the nation has no place or value (XI, 388-89).

We have earlier examined the role attributed by Veblen to nationalism and patriotism in the matter of social prog-ress: "the broad sands of patriotism" are the quicksands that swallow the constructive energies of the common man. The uses to which patriotism can be put are almost entirely deadly:

> . . . the patriotic sentiment never has been known to rise to the consummate pitch of enthusiastic abandon except when bent on some work of concerted malev-olence. Patriotism is of a contentious complexion, and finds its full expression in no other outlet than warlike enterprise; its highest and final appeal is for the death, damage, discomfort and destruction of the party of the second part.
>
> It is not that the spirit of patriotism will tolerate no other sentiments bearing on matters of public interest, but only that it will tolerate none that traverse the call of the national prestige (V, 33-34).

Veblen may seem too uncritical in his denunciation of patriotism and nationalism. Over the centuries nationalism has exacted an extraordinary toll of "death, damage, discomfort, and destruction." But nationalism, both in the past and the present, has also acted to unify and organize geographic areas, to enhance cultural achievements, and to serve as a great motor for fostering processes of economic and political development. All that may be so, whatever may be said of the cost. But Veblen may be correct when he argues that a distinction may and must be made between a "nation" and a "nationality."

A nation is an organization for collective offence and defence, in peace and war,—essentially based on hate and fear of other nations; a nationality is a cultural group, bound together by home-bred affinities of language, tradition, use and wont, and commonly also by a supposed community race,—essentially based on sympathies and sentiments of self-complacency within itself (VII, 147).

This distinction between "nation" and "nationality" may be too fine to be politically meaningful. But there are signs that such a distinction is gaining acceptance, and they are signs that warrant encouragement. Doubtless many present and potential difficulties are associated with the European Common Market, but it does represent the beginnings of a development consistent with Veblen's distinction. Much the same can be said of still embryonic attempts to develop regional economies in Asia, Africa, Latin America, and in the Arab world.

Veblen's distinction between the "nation" and "nationality" is based upon what he called the "invidiousness" of the nation as compared with the "community feeling" of the nationality. Both may perhaps be traced back to the needs and possibilities confronting families, tribes, and other forms of primitive organization in their savage and barbarian states. But civilization today, which is based upon industry, requires that the "invidious" inclinations of man be subdued and that his "community feelings" be heightened.

If, as is widely assumed today, war has become technologically outdated, Veblen would argue that for the same reasons the nation state has become outdated—whether on grounds of economic well-being or sheer survival. For Veblen, the representation of domestic business interests in foreign economic affairs was both a principal use of the nation state, and a principal source of "disturbance to the peace." It followed that peace in the world required a substantial curtailment of the prerogatives of business enterprise:

> . . . vested interests engaged in the pursuit of private gain in foreign parts, in the way of foreign investments, foreign concessions, export trade, and the like, . . . find the national establishment serviceable in enforcing claims and in procuring a profitably benevolent consideration of their craving for gain on the part of those foreign nations into whose jurisdiction their question of profits is driving them (XI, 389).

> . . . If the projectors of this peace at large are in any degree inclined to seek concessive terms on which the peace might hopefully be made enduring, it should evidently be a part of their endeavors from the outset to put events in train for the present abatement and eventual abrogation of the rights of ownership and of the price-system in which these rights take effect (V, 367).

The last chapter of *The Nature of Peace* is entitled "Peace and the Price System." Veblen came to the conclusion that it was "peace *or* the price system."

The power struggle of our time has formidable dimensions that Veblen did not foresee. Some aspects of that struggle are an outcome of fundamentally irrational attitudes, actions and expectations. Regarding these latter, Veblen's approach is most applicable and useful; and it may be offered that a substantial reduction of the "irrational dimensions" could make the remaining hard-core of conflict in the world more manageable in the sense that Veblen's ideas help us to know what may be *expected* from a particular relationship, and what is made *possible* under certain conditions. A brief examination of what may be expected from the Common Market, and what is possible in the underdeveloped countries, will illustrate this point. In both cases the problems and possibilities relating to technological and institutional change are central.

The European Common Market represents a substantial institutional change, made possible to a critical degree by a process combining rapid economic growth with technological improvement. The rapid growth supported, and was supported by a rational approach to the use of industrial technology—involving coordination and planning—taking place in a context of worldwide economic expansion, the replacement of a war-damaged and old-fashioned productive structure, and financial aid from the United States. In many and important ways, the industrial technology of the Common Market countries is superior to that in America: the process of technological borrowing, which once helped the United States to take the lead away from England, is now being reversed. Combined with her own substantial and independent innovations, Europe's technology now poses the threats of its possibilities.

Up to this point in time, the consequences of this European development have been largely beneficial to America and to those directly concerned. But the enormous productive capacity now in place in "Europe" will become a dangerous weapon, unless it continues to exist in an expanding world economy, especially as it is recognized that the American economy suffers from chronic excess capacity. Rising living standards in Europe and America can absorb some of this productive capacity if "social innovation" is assumed. But the principal source of continuing expansion in the world economy must rest upon the economic development of the presently non-industrial countries; and that requires the utmost in cooperation in the world economy.

For this development to happen, current notions of what is possible and what is necessary in the underdeveloped countries must be changed, and at least partially along Veblenian lines. What is possible rests upon Veblen's concept of the "advantage of coming late." What is necessary has at least two sides: 1) the necessity for sweeping institutional changes in the developing countries, and 2) institutional experimentation that subordinates "businesslike" to "industrial" criteria, both in the developing countries and in their external relationships. To appreciate both the "possible" and the "necessary" requires the shedding of traditional preconceptions in the advanced (and in the underdeveloped) countries; it also requires a more enlightened use of power and probably a different distribution of power.

Current attitudes toward the underdeveloped countries are strongly reminiscent of similar attitudes in the past. The Greeks scorned the Romans, who ultimately subdued them; the Romans gave way to the contemptible "barbarians"; the enlightened Arabs of the tenth century were appalled by the "pale, uncouth, and bearded" roughnecks of a hopelessly backward northwestern Europe; the "Europeans" gazed with haughtiness at the crudities of America; Americans proved to themselves that the Russians could not develop industrial strength; and today the industrialized peoples of the world believe that the institutions, the geography, the attitudes of Africans, Asians, and Latin Americans condemn them to permanent backwardness. Perhaps.

Such conceits have a long and honorable history; under genial conditions they might be a source of nothing more than amusement. In a world in which poverty and luxury stare at each other over a great divide, in which ideologies change and clash in desperate profusion, and in which nuclear warheads abound in the ocean, on land, and in the air—in such a world it is safer to give the benefit of the doubt; to assume that man, not fate, impedes development in the poor countries; to believe that where there's a will there's a way.

The process of economic development is not easily spurred,

even with the best of intentions and the best theories. But today the gateway to development is blocked by numerous obstacles. Not all, but some of the most important, of these obstacles are the residue of centuries of businesslike exploitation and misrule, put in place by the thoughtful and thoughtless activities of the presently industrialized nations. It is neither necessary nor possible to list and explain these obstacles here; suffice it to say, the "vicious circles of underdevelopment" are not more "natural" to the poor countries today than they were to the "underdeveloped countries" of the past. If today's developmental problems seem insurmountable, the peace and the prosperity of the entire world now requires that the attempt nonetheless be made to surmount those problems. If the past possessed many advantages not possessed by the present, the present has one immense advantage over the past. Industrial technology makes it *possible* to improve the conditions of life for all, not at the expense but to the benefit, of those already rich; indeed, the continuing welfare of the developed rich depends upon the steady progress of the underdeveloped poor.

Neither the neo-classical calculus of choice nor the capitalist calculus of profit is irrelevant if such progress is to occur; but the degree of their relevance is considerably less than they now enjoy in the discussions of economists and of policy-makers.

Looked at through Veblen's eyes, what are the probabilities that the present uses of mind and power will change in a more suitable direction? In attempting to answer this question we shall be led to raise some final questions concerning Veblen's strategic focus: namely, the relationships between instincts, institutions, and technological change.

Veblen pinned to the constructive "instincts" of workmanship and of idle curiosity whatever hopes he may have had for beneficial social change. Taken together, these propensities of man, which are the source of technological improvement and scientific understanding, are both enhanced by man's exposure to a "matter-of-fact" environment. Veblen was well aware that a man working with machinery, say, was affected by more than just that relationship; but he was convinced that continued exposure to the industrial mainstream would serve to erode, or at least to submerge, the "predatory instincts." Veblen saw man as the most cunning of animals because of his intelligence; he also saw that intelligence could be used for better or for worse. His hopes for man were based on the notion that prolonged exposure to industrialism and matter-of-fact life would help to pull man away from an irrational way of looking at things.

The closest that Veblen came to indicating what such a hopeful process might mean has frequently been interpreted as his "program." But the series of essays in which Veblen is thought to have put forth his "program of social reform" is not quite that. In those essays, *The Engineers and the Price System* (1921), Veblen mused on whether and how a society run by engineers might come about, how it might function, and what it would look like. Written at a time when Veblen's mood was one of dark despair, his position was not so much a program of action as an ironic statement of why such a program would be Utopian.

The American people, in their several capacities, are one by one ruled out as contributing to a sane and efficient society, either then or in the calculable future. Businessmen, who control the society through their power and prestige, are "incapable of anything like an effectual insight into the use of resources or the needs and aims of productive industry" (IX, 147). As for industrial workers, Veblen wrote:

> The nearest approach to a practicable organization of industrial forces in America, just yet, is the A.F. of L., which need only be named in order to dispel the illusion that there is anything to hope or fear in the way of a radical move at its hands. The A.F. of L. is itself one of the Vested Interests, as ready as any other to do battle for its own margin of privilege and profit (IX, 88).

Veblen took note of widespread grumbling in the population—e.g., as concerned with wartime profiteering and the highly unequal distribution of income—but he argued that the grumbling was based more on envy than on principled outrage:

> . . . apprehensive persons should not lose sight of the main fact that absentee ownership after all is the idol of every true American heart. . . . To achieve (or to inherit) a competency, that is to say to accumulate such wealth as will assure a "decent" livelihood in industrial *absentia,* is the universal, and universally laudable, ambition of all who have reached years of discretion; but it all means the same thing—to get something for nothing; at any cost (IX, 161-62).

Many of Veblen's readers, including some of his sympathizers, have assumed that he thought "the engineers" both could and would take over the economic system and make it run. The result would be "technocracy." Veblen did believe that modern industrial society required for its efficient management a guiding bureaucracy composed in part of those with technological training and ability. He also recognized the *potentially* powerful position held by "engineers," when he said "by themselves alone, the technicians can, in a few weeks, effectually incapacitate the country's productive industry . . ." (IX, 167).

Veblen was the least naïve of American social scientists on the sources and uses of political power in modern society; indeed, his view of the difficulties of change were the source of his pessimism. Consequently, while recognizing the strategic position of "technicians," he added two considerations: The technicians could not succeed in a revolutionary "strike" without "the tolerant consent of the population at large, backed by the aggressive support of the trained working force engaged in transportation and in the greater primary industries . . ." (IX, 167); and he closed his essays on the engineers with what can hardly be judged as a revolutionary prognosis:

> By way of conclusion it may be recalled again that, just yet, the production engineers are a scattering lot of fairly

contented subalterns, working piecemeal under orders from the deputies of the absentee owners; the working force of the great mechanical industries, including transportation, are still nearly out of touch and out of sympathy with the technical men, and are bound in rival trade organizations whose sole and self-seeking interest converges on the full dinner-pail; while the underlying population are as nearly uninformed on the state of things as the Guardians of the Vested Interests, including the commercialized newspapers, can manage to keep them, and they are consequently still in a frame of mind to tolerate no substantial abatement of absentee ownership; and the constituted authorities are competently occupied with maintaining the status quo. There is nothing in the situation that should reasonably flutter the sensibilities of the Guardians or of that massive body of well-to-do citizens who make up the rank and file of absentee owners, just yet (IX, 168-69).

"Just yet." The door is always left slightly ajar by Veblen. The basis for thinking it can open even wider requires an ironic approach to one of his basic concepts: namely, "conspicuous consumption." In Veblen's hands this concept is an outcome of his values, as well as a part of his economics.

A farm boy of the late nineteenth century, Veblen developed complicated and intense intellectual interests. He was raised in simplicity and felt at home with simplicity all his life. The urban society of which he became a part was blatant and vulgar and crudely unjust. The few who could easily afford it wasted much on lavish display, while the majority that worked very hard for very little emulated the few. The "conspicuous consumption" that gave rise to Veblen's concept was composed of servants, gaudy architecture, and luxurious personal and interior decoration—"elaborate and cumbrous, in the way of dwellings, furniture, bric-a-brac, wardrobe and meals. . . ." (I, 65-66). The technology that produced these goods and services was not, in Veblen's own terms, modern. The goods that now underlie conspicuous consumption (and that did in Veblen's last years) are industrially produced: automobiles, washers and dryers, books, records, and the like. These are mass-produced goods, and they are consumed, new and used, by the masses. The process through which these products have come to be produced and used in the mass has lived up to Veblen's expectation: it has been sustained by advertising and emulation, and it has gone far to trivialize social behavior and attitudes. There is more to be said, however, and Veblen did not quite say it.

First, one need not be driven by emulation or goaded by advertising to believe that the gas stove is preferable to the wood stove, machine-washing to hand-washing, modern housing to the log cabin, frozen orange juice to no orange juice. Indeed, the entire world is astir with the desire for some approximation to the "American standard of living"; and if some of this stirring is due to emulation, and some to propaganda, its hard center is made of the desire to live comfortably and safely, once such possibilities appear on the horizon. Nor is it coincidental that widespread health and literacy are just as much the preserve of the conspicuously consuming countries as are TV sets, wall-to-wall carpeting, and gilded automobiles.

Second, more to the point, and in keeping with Veblen's own economics, a "genetic analysis" reveals something that Veblen overlooked. America is the birthplace of the hard sell, the soft sell, the subliminal sell. But America is also the birthplace of modern mass-production techniques; it is the birthplace of the technological possibilities which, if they threaten to destroy us in spirit and in body, are also our main source of hope that both spirit and body can survive and flourish. The roots even of the flower are sunk in dirt. The existence of current technological possibilities is an outcome of both the sensible and nonsensical characteristics of American economic development; each contributed to the other at each step on the way to the present. Future developmental processes need not follow the same path; but that is in large part because we have come to where we are, by *our* path.

Veblen knew his economic history as well as any; he knew

that the industrialism he admired was wrung from what he detested: the anguish, the privation, the greed, the violence, the bloodshed of long centuries. If on that past this present must rest, on this present a more civilized future can grow. Ideas and ethical standards are a prime requisite for such a development; modern technology is the necessary condition for constructive ideas and ethics to become operational. Veblen knew that ethics and scarcity were enemies; we may hope that abundance and ethics are mutually reinforcing.

But more than good thoughts are necessary. It is one thing to say that the productivity of modern industry, whatever its roots, makes possible a new approach to social institutions. It is quite another thing to lose sight of the roots. In the spirit of Veblen—where "spirit" includes his hopes, his fears, and his analysis—"what's next" is most likely to be determined by what *is*. Today that includes still a population "as nearly uninformed on the state of things as the Guardians of the Vested Interests can manage to keep them," made up of "fairly contented subalterns," unwilling to tolerate any "substantial abatement of absentee ownership," and quite able to view with calm frequent appeals "for the death, damage, discomfort and destruction of the party of the second part."

Others are repelled by the world's violence to mind and body, by the ugly and dangerous contrast between luxurious living for the few and desperate poverty for the mass of humanity. Many perceive and reject the mindless procession toward the garrison state that, if it moves at different paces, knows no boundaries. Many wish to build a bridge between scarcity and abundance, to use the wonders of technology to obliterate poverty, and believe that the alternative is the obliteration of civilization.

For such as these Veblen and his work have continuing relevance. In a deep sense, Veblen is the most American of social scientists: his life and his work are paradoxical. More than others, Veblen took seriously the values that have made America a shining symbol to the rest of the world: democracy, freedom, well-being, peace. More than others, Veblen showed that the institutions prized by Americans are means that must be questioned lest they become ends in themselves, tarnish our values, and render us corrupt. Veblen had no panacea for our sickness, but he enabled us to perceive its causes.

Appendix on

THE HIGHER LEARNING IN AMERICA

Veblenisms

I have deliberately chosen this disjointed way of presenting Veblen's views on higher education. Veblen had something important to say about education, and he said it in a specialized "monograph." Since I view Veblen primarily as being an economist, I have concentrated on his approach to economic problems and economic theory. To have fitted his views on higher education into this framework would have been forced and awkward; to have neglected them would have been to overlook one of Veblen's most valuable contributions.

Veblen was a scholar and a scientist first before he became a specialist in economics. His scholarly inclination was so pronounced that it may have enabled him to dwell as he did on the "instinct of idle curiosity." *The Higher Learning*, which takes "the instinct of idle curiosity" as its starting point, is Veblen's most heartfelt book and it establishes his belief that the pursuit of truth is the essence of the good life; without it, there is no good life at all.

As a college professor, Veblen knew American universities well. He taught all over the country for a generation or so. What he experienced and what he knew of the life and drift of university life in America led him to see its "heart being eaten out." The monster devouring the heart was business control of universities through governing boards, with ramifications down through the president (the "captain of erudition"), the deans, and a whole string of associated paraphernalia created and encouraged by the ruling powers —an inane grading system, fraternities, "ceremonial dissipation," and much else indicated below.

Veblen did not view all this as the result of a vast conspiracy; it was what one must expect in a society so thoroughly captivated by business criteria. But one could not expect that the pursuit of truth could be carried out well or fully within an atmosphere cluttered up by the irrelevant and inimical institutions engendered by business influence. More than that, in Veblen's time a move had already begun to set up research institutes in which the pursuit of truth could go on unhindered by the fripperies, foolishness, and constraints of the diluted undergraduate-graduate instruction in America. This effort he saw as destructive not only of the heart of the university, but also of the disinterested and effective pursuit of truth—if for no other reason than that the pursuit of truth requires that scholars be surrounded by inquiring students, themselves incipient scholars.

The long series of quotations below from *The Higher Learning* allows Veblen to speak for himself, and to do so in a structure of argument, illustration, and conclusion. The entire book must be read, however, to appreciate fully Veblen's position.

THE HIGHER LEARNING; UNIVERSITY, COLLEGE AND PROFESSIONAL SCHOOL; SCHOLARSHIP AND TEACHING

For good or ill, civilized men have come to hold that [the] matter-of-fact knowledge of things is the only end in life that indubitably justifies itself. So that nothing more irretrievably shameful could overtake modern civilization than the miscarriage of this modern learning, which is the most valued spiritual asset of mankind (p. 8).

It is always possible, of course, that this pre-eminence of intellectual enterprise in the civilization of the Western peoples is a transient episode; that it may eventually—perhaps even precipitately, with the next impending turn in the fortunes of this civilization—again be relegated to a secondary place in the scheme of things and become only an instrumentality in the service of some dominant aim or impulse, such as a vainglorious patriotism, or dynastic politics, or the breeding of a commercial aristocracy. . . . But hitherto the spokesmen of any such cultural reversion are careful to declare a perfunctory faith in that civilization of disinterested intellectual achievement which they are endeavouring to suborn to their several ends. That such *pro forma* declarations are found necessary argues that the faith in a civilization of intelligence is still so far intact as to require all reactionaries to make their peace with it (p. 9).

The university is the only accepted institution of the modern culture on which the quest of knowledge unquestionably devolves; and the visible drift of circumstances as well as of public sentiment runs also to making this the only unquestioned duty incumbent on the university (p. 11).

The conservation and advancement of the higher learning involves two lines of work, distinct but closely bound together: (a) scientific and scholarly inquiry, and (b) the instruction of students. The former of these is primary and indispensable. It is this work of intellectual enterprise that gives its character to the university and marks it off from the lower schools. The work of teaching properly belongs in the university only because and in so far as it incites and facilitates the university man's work of inquiry,—and the extent to which such teaching furthers the work of inquiry is scarcely to be appreciated without a somewhat extended experience. . . . Teaching, as a concomitant of investigation, is distinctly advantageous to the investigator; particularly in so far as his work is of the nature of theoretical inquiry (p. 12).

University teaching, having a particular and special purpose—the pursuit of knowledge—has also a particular and special character, such as to differentiate it from other teaching and at the same time leave it relatively ineffective for

[161]

other purposes. Its aim is to equip the student for the work of inquiry, not to give him facility in that conduct of affairs that turns such knowledge to "practical account." . . . The university man is, properly, a student, not a schoolmaster (p. 13).

The scientist and the scholar on the one hand, and the schoolmaster on the other hand, both belong within the later growth of civilization; but a differentiation of the two classes, and a division of their work, is indispensable if they are to do their work as it should be done, and as the modern community thoughtfully intends that it should be done. And while such a division of labor has hitherto not been carried through with any degree of consistency, it is at least under way, and there is nothing but the presumption of outworn usage that continues to hold the two lines of work together, to the detriment of both; backed, it is true, by ambitions of self-aggrandisement on the part of many schools and many of their directorates (p. 14).

. . . while the university should offer no set curriculum, the college has, properly, nothing else to offer. But the retention or inclusion of the college and its aims within the university corporation has necessarily led to the retention of college standards and methods of control even in what is or purports to be university work; so that it is by no means unusual to find university [graduate] work scheduled in the form of a curriculum, with all that boarding-school circumstance and apparatus that is so unavoidable an evil in all undergraduate training. In effect, the outcome of these shortsighted attempts to take care of the higher learning by the means and method of the boys' school, commonly is to eliminate the higher learning from the case and substitute the aims and results of a boys' training school (p. 18).

It is true that, by historical accident, the university at large has grown out of professional training-schools,—primarily schools for training in theology, secondarily in law and medicine. It is also true, in like wise and like degree, that modern science and scholarship have grown out of the technology of handicraft and the theological philosophy of the schoolmen. But just as it would be a bootless enterprise to cut modern science back into handicraft technology, so would it be a gratuitous imbecility to prune back the modern university to that inchoate phase of its life-history and make it again a corporation for the training of theologians, jurists and doctors of medicine. The historical argument does not enjoin a return to the beginning of things, but rather an intelligent appreciation of what things are coming to (p. 24).

THE BUSINESS OF EDUCATION

The cult of the idle curiosity sticks too deep in the instinctive endowment of the race, and it has in modern civilization been too thoroughly ground into the shape of a quest of matter-of-fact knowledge, to allow this pursuit to be definitively set aside or to fall into abeyance. It is by too much an integral constituent of the habits of thought induced by the discipline of workday life . . . to admit of its supersession by any objective end alien to it,—at least for the present and until some stronger force than the technological discipline of modern life shall take over the primacy among the factors of civilization, and so give us a culture of a different character from that which has brought on this modern science and placed it at the centre of things human (p. 111).

Distinctive and dominant among the constituent factors of [the] current scheme of use and wont is the pursuit of business, with the outlook and predilections which that pursuit implies. Therefore any inquiry into the effect which recent institutional changes may have upon the pursuit of the higher learning will necessarily be taken up in a peculiar degree with the consequences which an habitual pursuit of business in modern times has had for the ideals, aims and methods of the scholars and schools devoted to the higher learning (p. 3).

. . . while the higher learning still remains as the enduring purpose and substantial interest of the university establishment, the dominant practical interests of the day will, transiently but effectually, govern the detail lines of academic policy, the range of instruction offered, and the character of the personnel; and more particularly and immediately will the character of the governing boards and the academic administration so be determined by the current run of popular sentiment touching the community's practical needs and aims; since these ruling bodies stand, in one way or another, under the critical surveillance of a lay constituency (p. 45).

The incursion of business principles into the academic community is also of relatively recent date, and should not yet have had time to pervade the organization throughout and with full effect; so that the regime of competitive strategy should as yet be neither so far advanced nor so secure a matter of course as may fairly be expected in the near future. Yet the rate of advance along this line, and the measure of present achievement, are more considerable than even a very sanguine advocate of business principles could have dared to look for a couple of decades ago (p. 70).

GOVERNING BOARDS, CAPTAINS OF ERUDITION, AND DEANS

Plato's classic scheme of folly, which would have the philosophers take over the management of affairs, has been turned on its head; the men of affairs have taken over the direction of the pursuit of knowledge. To anyone who will take a dispassionate look at this modern arrangement it looks foolish, of course,—ingeniously foolish; but, also, of course, there is no help for it and no prospect of its abatement in the calculable future. . . . Its institutional ground is the current system of private ownership (p. 57).

For a generation past, while the American universities have been coming into line as seminaries of the higher learning, there has gone on a wide-reaching substitution of laymen in the place of clergymen on the governing boards. This progressive secularization is sufficiently notorious, even though there are some among the older establishments the terms of whose charters require a large proportion of clergymen on their boards. This secularization is entirely consonant with the prevailing drift of sentiment in the community at large, as is shown by the uniform and uncritical approval with which it is regarded. The substitution is a substitution of businessmen and politicians; which amounts to saying that it is a substitution of businessmen. So that the discretionary control in matters of university policy now [1918] rests finally in the hands of businessmen (p. 46).

. . . these businesslike governing boards commonly exercise little if any current surveillance of the corporate affairs of the university, beyond a directive oversight of the distribution of expenditures among the several academic purposes for which the corporate income is to be used; that is to say, they control the budget of expenditures; which comes to saying that they exercise a pecuniary discretion in the case mainly in the way of deciding what the body of academic men that constitutes the university may or may not do with the means in hand; that is to say, their pecuniary surveillance comes in the main to an interference with the academic work, the merits of which these men of affairs on the governing board are in no special degree qualified to judge. Beyond this, as touches the actual running administration of the corporation's investments, income and expenditures,— all that is taken care of by permanent officials who have, as they necessarily must, sole and responsible charge of these matters (p. 47).

Except for the insuperable difficulty of getting a hearing for such an extraordinary proposal, it should be no difficult matter to show that these governing boards of businessmen commonly are quite useless to the university for any businesslike purpose. Indeed, except for a stubborn prejudice to the contrary, the fact should readily be seen that the boards are of no material use in any connection; their sole effectual function being to interfere with the academic management in matters that are not of the nature of business, and that lie outside their competence and outside the range of their habitual interest (p. 48).

. . . the higher administrative officials . . . will commonly occupy an advanced academic rank, and so will take a high (putative) rank as scholars and scientists. . . . They will be selected on the same general grounds of fitness as their chief,—administrative facility, plausibility, proficiency as public speakers and parliamentarians, ready versatility of convictions, and a staunch loyalty to their bread. Experience teaches that scholarly or scientific capacity does not enter in any appreciable measure among the qualifications so required for responsible academic office, beyond what may thriftily serve to mask the conventional decencies of the case (p. 69).

THE STUDENT

The student who comes up to the university for the pursuit of knowledge is expected to know what he wants and to want it, without compulsion. If he falls short in these respects, if he has not the requisite interest and initiative, it is his own misfortune, not the fault of his teacher. What he has a legitimate claim to is an opportunity for such personal contact and guidance as will give him familiarity with the ways and means of the higher learning,—any information imparted to him being incidental to this main work of habituation. He gets a chance to make himself a scholar, and what he will do with his opportunities in this way lies in his own discretion (p. 14).

. . . *bona fide* students will require but little exacting surveillance in their work, and little in the way of an apparatus of control. But the collegiate school has to deal with a large body of students, many of whom have little abiding interest in their academic work, beyond the academic credits necessary to be accumulated for honorable discharge,—indeed their scholastic interest may fairly be said to center in unearned credits.

For this reason, and also because of the difficulty of controlling a large volume of perfunctory labor, such as is involved in undergraduate instruction, the instruction offered must be reduced to standard units of time, grade and volume. Each unit of work required, or rather of credit allowed, in this mechanically drawn scheme of tasks must be the equivalent of all the other units; otherwise a comprehensive system of scholastic accountancy will not be practicable, and injustice and irritation will result both among the pupils and the schoolmasters. For the greater facility and accuracy in conducting this scholastic accountancy, as well as with a view to the greater impressiveness of the published schedule of courses offered, these mechanical units of academic bullion are increased in number and decreased in weight and volume; until the parcelment and mechanical balance of units reaches a point not easily credible to any outsider who might naïvely consider the requirements of scholarship to be an imperative factor in academic administration (p. 75-76).

. . . the standards set up in this scholastic accountancy are high and rigorous; in application, the exactions of the credit system must not be enforced in so inflexible a spirit as to estrange that much-desired contingent of genteel students whose need of an honorable discharge is greater than their love of knowledge. Neither must its demands on the student's time and energy be allowed seriously to interfere with those sports and "student activities" that make up the chief attraction of college life for a large proportion of the university's young men, and that are, in the apprehension of

[167]

many, so essential a part in the training of the modern gentlemen (p. 76).

Well to the front among [the] undergraduate appurtenances of gentlemanship are the factional clubs known as Greek-letter fraternities. These touch the province of learning in the universities only incidentally and superficially, as they do not in practice enter the graduate division except by way of a thin aftermath of factional animus, which may occasionally infect such of the staff as are gifted with a particularly puerile temperament. They are, in effect, competitive organizations for the elaboration of the puerile irregularities of adolescence . . . (p. 89-90).

THE FACULTY

A wise academic policy, conducted by an executive looking to the fiscal interests of the university, will aim not to alienate the affections of the large businessmen of a ripe age, by harboring specialists whose inquiries are likely to traverse these old-settled convictions in the social, economic, political, or religious domain. It is bad business policy to create unnecessary annoyance. So it comes about that the habitual munificence of the captains of industry who have reached their term will have grave consequences for that range of academic science that is occupied with matters on which they hold convictions. . . . Remotely by force of a worldly-wise appointing power, proximately by force of the good taste and sober sense of well-chosen incumbents, something of a filial piety comes to pervade the academic handling of those institutional phenomena that touch the sentiments of the passing generation (p. 135).

Distempered critics have even alleged that the academic leaders in the social sciences are held under some constraint, as being, in some sort, in the pay of the well-to-do conservative element. . . . Now, it may be conceded without violence to notorious facts, that these official leaders of science do commonly reach conclusions innocuous to the existing law and order, particularly with respect to religion, ownership, and the distribution of wealth. But this need imply no constraint, nor even any peculiar degree of tact, much less a moral obliquity. . . . [Social scientists] are free to give the fullest expression to any conclusions or convictions to which their inquiries may carry them. That they are able to do so is a fortunate circumstance, due to the fact that their intellectual horizon is bounded by the same limits of commonplace insight and preconceptions as are the prevailing opinions of the conservative middle class. That is to say, a large and aggressive mediocrity is the prime qualification for a leader of science in these lines, if his leadership is to gain academic authentication (p. 135-36).

As bearing on this whole matter of pomp and circumstance, social amenities and ritual dissipation, quasi-learned demonstrations and meretricious publicity, in academic life, it is difficult beyond hope of a final answer to determine how much of it is due directly to the masterful initiative of the strong man who directs the enterprise, and how much is to be set down to an innate proclivity for all that sort of thing on the part of the academic personnel. A near view of these phenomena leaves the impression that there is, on the whole, less objection felt than expressed among the academic men with regard to this routine of demonstration; that the reluctance with which they pass under the ceremonial yoke is not altogether ingenuous; all of which would perhaps hold true even more decidedly as applied to the faculty households.*

* The share and value of the "faculty wives" in all this routine of resolute conviviality is a large topic, an intelligent and veracious account of which could only be a work of naïve brutality (p. 123).

Broadly speaking, no requirement of the academic routine should be allowed to stand in the way of an available occasion for a scholastic pageant (p. 115).

. . . an intimate familiarity with current academic life is calculated to raise the question whether make-believe does not, after all, occupy a larger and more urgent place in the life of these thoughtful adult male citizens than in the life of their children (p. 123).

THE ARCHITECTURE

Out of the past comes the conventional preconception that . . . scholastic edifices should show something of the revered traits of ecclesiastical and monastic real estate; while out of the present comes an ingrained predilection for the more sprightly and exuberant forms of decoration and magnificence to which the modern concert hall, the more expensive cafés and clubrooms, and the Pullman coaches have given a degree of authentication. . . . It is not necessary here to offer many speculations on the enduring artistic merit of these costly stage properties of the seats of learning, since their permanent value in that respect is scarcely to be rated as a substantial motive in their construction. . . . But there is another side to this architecture of notoriety, that merits some slight further remark. It is consistently and unavoidably meretricious. . . [,] which may suggest reflections on the fitness of housing the quest of truth in an edifice of false pretences (p. 105-06).

THE SCHOLARLY REFUGE

[The] evidence goes to say that the difficulties of the academic situation are insurmountable; any rehabilitation of the universities is not contemplated in [the] latterday movement . . . designed to shift the seat of the higher learning out of the precincts of the schools. And it is so coming to be recognized, in effect though tacitly, that for all their professions of a singleminded addiction to the pursuit of learning, the academic establishments, old and new, are no longer competent to take the direction of affairs in this domain.

So it is that, with a sanguine hope born of academic defeat, there have latterly been founded certain large establishments, of the nature of retreats or shelters for the prosecution of scientific and scholarly inquiry in some sort of academic quarantine, detached from all academic affiliation and renouncing all share in the work of instruction. . . . This move looks like a desperate surrender of the university ideal (p. 199).

It is . . . impracticable and inadvisable to let . . . institutions of research take over any appreciable share of that work of scientific and scholarly instruction that is slipping out of the palsied hands of the universities, so as to include some consistent application to teaching within the scope of their everyday work. And this cuts out of their complement of ways and means one of the chief aids to an effectual pursuit of scientific inquiry. Only in the most exceptional, not to say erratic, cases will good, consistent, sane and alert scientific work be carried forward through a course of years by any scientist without [graduate] students, without loss or blunting of that intellectual initiative that makes the creative scientist (p. 200).

Meantime, that which is eating the heart out of the American seminaries of the higher learning should in due course also work out the like sterilization in the universities of Europe, as fast and as far as these other countries also come fully into line with the same pecuniary ideals that are making the outcome in America. . . . America is by no means in a unique position in this matter, except only in respect of the eminent degree in which this community is pervaded by business principles, and its consequent faith in businesslike methods, and its intolerance of any other than pecuniary standards of value. It is only that this country is in the lead; the other peoples of Christendom are following the same lead as fast as their incumbrance of archaic usages and traditions will admit; and the generality of their higher schools are already beginning to show the effects of the same businesslike aspirations, decoratively colored with feudalistic archaisms of patriotic buncombe (p. 201).

SOME PROPOSALS

To the substantial gain of both parties, though with some lesion of the vanity of both, the separation between the university and the professional and technical schools should be carried through and made absolute. Only on such conditions can either the one or the other do its own work in a workmanlike manner. Within the university precincts any aim or interest other than those of irresponsible science and scholarship—pursuit of matter-of-fact knowledge—are to be rated as interlopers (p. 23).

If, then, as indications run, the large undergraduate schools are in due course to develop somewhat unreservedly into gentlemen's colleges, that is an additional reason why, in the interest of both parties, the divorce of the university from the collegiate division should be made absolute. Neither does the worldly spirit that pervades the gentlemen's college further the university's interest in scholarship, nor do the university's scholarly interests further the college work in gentility (p. 89).

. . . workday habituation under the stress of competitive business has induced a frame of mind that will tolerate no other method of procedure, and no rule of life that does not approve itself as a faithful travesty of competitive enterprise. And since the quest of learning cannot be carried on by the methods or with the apparatus and incidents of competitive business, it follows that the only remedial measures that hold any promise of rehabilitation for the higher learning in the universities cannot be attempted in the present state of public sentiment.

All that is required is the abolition of the academic executive and of the governing board. Anything short of this heroic remedy is bound to fail, because the evils sought to be remedied are inherent in these organs, and intrinsic to their functioning (p. 202).

It is not intended, seriously and as a practical measure, to propose the abolition of the president's office, or of the governing board; nor is it intended to intimate that the captain of erudition can be dispensed with in fact. He is too dear to the commercialized popular imagination, and he fits too convincingly into the businessmen's preconceived scheme of things, to permit any such sanguine hope of surcease from skilled malpractice and malversation. All that is here intended to be said is nothing more than the *obiter dictum* that, as seen from the point of view of the higher learning, the academic executive and all his works are anathema, and should be discontinued by the simple expedient of wiping him off the slate; and that the governing board, in so far as it presumes to exercise any other than vacantly perfunctory duties, has the same value and should with advantage be lost in the same shuffle (p. 209).

Veblenisms

SALESMANSHIP

It is of the nature of sales-publicity, to promise much and deliver a minimum. *Suppresio veri, suggestio falsi.* Worked out to its ideal finish, as in the promises and performance of the publicity-agents of the Faith, it should be the high good fortune of the perfect salesman in the secular field also to promise everything and deliver nothing (X, 321-22).

Human credulity appears to be peculiarly tractable under the pressure of a well-conceived appeal to fear and shame, and to set into obstinate and extraordinary shapes (action patterns) on relatively slight habituation along these lines. The fear and shame on which the sales-publicity proceeds in its work of turning credulous persons into profitable customers are the fear of mortal disease and the fear of losing prestige (X, 310).

SPORTS

. . . addiction to sport of one kind and another and preoccupation with sportsmanlike interests and values has spread from the levels of gentility down through the body of the population, until this category of dissipations has become almost the sole ground of common interest on which working-men meet or hold opinions (IV, 148).

It is quite beyond the reach of imagination that any adult male citizen would of his own motion go in for the elaborate futilities of British shooting or horse racing, e.g., or for such a *tour de force* of inanity as polo, or mountain climbing, or expeditions after big game. The deadening of the sense of proportion implied in addiction to this round of infantile make-believe is not to be achieved in one generation; it needs to have all the authenticity that tradition can give it, and then its inculcation in the incoming generation must be begun in infancy and followed up throughout the educational system (IV, 142-43).

Sportsmen—hunters and anglers—are more or less in the habit of assigning a love of nature, the need of recreation, and the like, as the incentives to their favorite pastime. These motives are no doubt frequently present and make up a part of the attractiveness of the sportsman's life; but these cannot be the chief incentives. These ostensible needs could be more readily and fully satisfied without the accompaniment of a systematic effort to take the life of those creatures that make up an essential feature of that "nature" that is beloved by sportsmen (I, 257).

THE DYNASTIC STATE

The [German] system has the faults of its qualities, and among its qualities are not amiability, toleration, and ingenuousness. A dynastic State cannot be set afloat in the milk of human kindness (IV, 216).

In the Fatherland the commercial and industrial classes have been called on to play their part without time to learn their lines (V, 194).

It is as difficult for the commonplace Englishman to understand what the German means by the "State" as it is for the German to comprehend the English conception of a "commonwealth," or very nearly so (IV, 160).

The truth and beauty of a regime of dynastic usufruct is not realized in the absence of a suitable background of war and rapine. . . . [When so conceived], the uses of a dynastic establishment are seen to be of the same nature as the uses of a tapeworm; and the tapeworm's relation to his host is something not easy to beautify in words, or even to authenticate in such convincing fashion as will insure his affectionate retention on grounds of decorous use and wont (IV, 168-69).

It may be true that, for the present, on critical or weighty measures the parliamentary discretion [in Germany] extends no farther than respectfully to say: 'Ja wohl!' But then, Ja wohl is also something; and there is no telling where it may all lead to in the long course of years (V, 191).

ARMAMENTS AND WAR

Any politician who succeeds in embroiling his country in a war, however nefarious, becomes a popular hero and is reputed a wise and righteous statesman, at least for the time being. Illustrative instances need perhaps not, and indeed cannot gracefully, be named; most popular heroes and reputed statesmen belong in this class (V, 22).

The great business interests are the more inclined to look kindly on an extension of warlike enterprise and armaments, since the pecuniary advantages inure to them, while the pecuniary burden falls chiefly on the rest of the community. It is, to say the least, highly improbable that the business gains which accrue from a well-conducted foreign policy ever, in modern times, equal the cost at which they are secured; but that consideration scarcely enters, since the costs are not paid out of business gains, but out of the industry of the rest of the people. The people, however, are animated with an uncritical persuasion that they have some sort of a residuary share in these gains, and that this residuary share in some manner exceeds the whole of the gains secured (II, 297n).

Preparation for the common defense . . . appears unfailingly to eventuate in hostilities. . . . In proportion as the resulting equipment for defense grows great and becomes formidable, the range of items which a patriotically biased nation are ready to include among the claims to be defended grows incontinently larger, until by the overlapping of defensive claims between rival nationalities the distinction between defense and aggression disappears, except in the biased fancy of the rival patriots (V, 62).

. . . loss of moral perspective through an overweening sense of power appears to follow equally whether the stronger is or is not superior in any other respect,—perhaps even more pronouncedly in the latter case. . . . It is the moral attitude of the pot-hunter towards the fur-bearing animals. One does not keep faith with the fur-bearing animals (IV, 256n).

The comprehensive and exacting demands of universal military service as it applies to the population at large have

had . . . [the] effect on the common man . . . of diverting interest from the make-believe of sports to that of war;
and it is not at all certain that the loss to industry from
this cause, considerable as it has unquestionably been, has
not been fully offset by the greater docility of the working
classes resulting from their experience of surveillance and
subjection in the army. A military organization is necessarily
a servile organization, and the discipline of servile obedience
will always have its effect (IV, 247).

Such experience of irresponsible outrage and irremediable
calamity as is brought on by war has also the effect of
driving the men (and women) exposed to it into recourse
to magical and supernatural aid,—the futility of which is
only known, not proven. With ill-concealed glee the clergy
are already calling attention to a recrudescence of religious
superstition among the troops engaged on both sides in the
current [1915] campaign, and the like evidence that common sense is being superseded by spasmodic sentiment is
to be seen also among the unfortunate ones left at home,
whose addiction to devout observances is said to have greatly increased. Of much the same bearing, by some sort of
inversion or repercussion, is also the notably increased volume of profanity in which, it is credibly reported, the ostensible unbelievers are seeking refuge from their sense of
helplessness and incurable wrong (IV, 276n).

[Officers are presumably] men peculiarly fit for warlike
enterprise, and so presumably unfit for the arts of peace.
Also, whatever may be the case in respect of their congenital
fitness for war, it should be noted that officers commonly
are gentlemen, in the several senses which that word con-
veys; and gentlemen commonly have no industrial value.
Indeed, as bears on the net industrial efficiency of the community they have appreciably less than no value, being
typically unproductive consumers. The mortality among the
officers may therefore be set down as net gain, in the economic respect; and since they will at an average be highly
efficient consumers, their demise should count as an economic

relief to the community at large, and count at something more than a mere per capita rating (IV, 277).

The cultural effects of the discipline of warfare and armament are much the same whether it is undertaken for dynastic or for business ends; in either case it takes on a dynastic complexion and breeds the temperament, ideals, and institutional habits proper to a dynastic system of politics. The farther it goes the more it comes to make use of business interests as a means rather than as an end . . . (II, 299-300).

. . . in the present case the decision, or the choice, lies between two alternatives: either the price-system and its attendant business enterprise will yield and pass out; or the pacific nations will conserve their pecuniary scheme of law and order at the cost of returning to a war footing and letting their owners preserve the rights of ownership by force of arms (V, 366).

BUSINESS VERSUS INDUSTRY

The slave-trade never was a "nice" occupation or an altogether unexceptionable investment—"balanced on the edge of the permissible." But even though it may have been distasteful to one and another of its New-England men of affairs, and though there always was a suspicion of moral obliquity attached to the slave-trade, yet it had the fortune to be drawn into the service of the greater good. In conjunction with its running-mate, the rum-trade, it laid the foundations of some very reputable fortunes at that focus of commercial enterprise that presently became the center of American culture, and so gave rise to some of the country's Best People. At least so they say.

Perhaps also it was, in some part, in this early pursuit of gain in this moral penumbra that American business enterprise learned how not to let its right hand know what its left hand is doing; and there is always something to be done that is best done with the left hand (X, 171*n*).

The institutional animus of ownership, as it took shape under the discipline of early modern handicraft, awards the ownership of property to the workman who has produced it. By a dialectical conversion of the terms, this metaphysical dictum is made to fit the circumstances of later competitive business by construing acquisition of property to mean production of wealth; so that a businessman is looked upon as the putative producer of whatever wealth he acquires (II, 290-91).

As someone with a taste for slang and aphorism has said. . . , "In the beginning the Captain of Industry set out to do something, and in the end he sat down to do somebody" (X, 113).

In common with other men, the businessman is moved by ideals of serviceability and an aspiration to make the way of life easier for his fellows. Like other men, he has something of the instinct of workmanship. No doubt such aspirations move the great businessman less urgently than many others, who are, on that account, less successful in business affairs. Motives of this kind detract from business efficiency, and an undue yielding to them on the part of businessmen is to be deprecated as an infirmity (II, 41).

"He either fears his fate too much, Or his deserts are small, Who dare not put it to the touch" and take a chance with the legalities and the moralities . . . when there is easy money in sight and no one is looking, particularly in case his own solvency—that is his life as a business concern—should be in the balance. Solvency is always a meritorious work, however it may be achieved or maintained; and so long as one is quite sound on this main count one is sound on the whole, and can afford to forget peccadillos, within reason (X, 158).

. . . there is a formal limit on profitable evasion [of the rules], beyond which tact and salesmanship cease to be sportsmanlike finesse or businesslike ambiguity and become sharp practice or swindle.*

* It is not easy in any given case—indeed it is at times impossible until the courts have spoken—to say whether it is an instance of praise-worthy salesmanship or a penitentiary offense. All that may turn on a point of legal verbiage, and it may also depend somewhat on the magnitude of the transaction and the business rating of the parties in interest; a large transaction is, on the whole, less likely to be found reprehensible (X, 123).

The industrial system requires that the management and the industrial man power should be engaged on an increasingly close teamwork in production; in effect and increasingly, on grounds of sound business they are giving much of their attention to teamwork in sabotage (X, 297).

By settled habit the technicians, the engineers and industrial experts, are a harmless and docile sort, well fed on the whole, and somewhat placidly content with the "full dinner-pail" which the lieutenants of the Vested Interests habitually allow them (IX, 135).

The shrewd worldly wisdom of the businesslike managers, looking consistently to the main chance, works in harmoniously with their trained ignorance on matters of technology, to bring about what amounts to effectual teamwork for the defeat of the country's industrial system as a going concern. . . . It is true, the industrial system is continually growing, in volume and complication; and with every new extension of its scope and range, and with every added increment of technological practice that goes into effect, there comes a new and urgent opportunity for the businessmen in control to extend and speed up their strategy of mutual obstruction and defeat; it is all in the day's work (IX, 116-17).

. . . the common practice has come to be partial employment of equipment and man power on terms satisfactory to the owners; often rising to something near full employment for a limited time, but always with the reservation that the owner retains his legal right to withhold his property from productive use in whole or in part. Plainly, ownership would be nothing better than an idle gesture without this legal right of sabotage. Without the power of discretionary idleness, without the right to keep the work out of the hands of the workmen and the product out of the market, investment and business enterprise would cease. This is the larger meaning of the Security of Property (X, 66-67).

. . . competition as it runs under the rule of this decayed competitive system is chiefly between the business concerns that control production, on the one side, and the consuming public on the other side; the chief expedients in this businesslike competition being salesmanship and sabotage. Salesmanship in this connection means little else than prevarication, and sabotage means a businesslike curtailment of output (X, 78).

. . . if the country's productive industry were competently organized as a systematic whole, and were then managed by competent technicians with an eye single to maximum production of goods and services; instead of, as now, being manhandled by ignorant businessmen with an eye single to maximum profits; the resulting output of goods and services would doubtless exceed the current output by several hundred per cent (IX, 120-21).

It is not possible, on sound business grounds, to let the industrial forces of the country go to work and produce what, in the physical sense, the country needs; because a free run of production would, it is believed, be ruinous for business; because it would lower prices and so reduce the net business gain below the danger point—the point below which the fixed charges on outstanding obligations would not be covered by the net returns. Hence what is conveniently called capitalistic sabotage or businesslike sabotage on industry (X, 96).

Now, these businesslike manoeuvres of deviation and delay are by no means to be denounced as being iniquitous or unfair, although they may have an unfortunate effect on the conditions of life for the common man. That is his misfortune, which law and custom count on his bearing with becoming fortitude (VII, 94).

. . . the spirit of venturesome enterprise is [now] more than likely to foot up as a hunting of trouble, and wisdom in business enterprise has more and more settled down to the wisdom of "watchful waiting."*

* Doubtless this form of words, "watchful waiting," will have been employed in the first instance to describe the frame of mind of a toad who has reached years of discretion and has found his appointed place along some frequented run where many flies and spiders pass and repass on their way to complete that destiny to which it has pleased an all-seeing and merciful Providence to call them; but by an easy turn of speech it has also been found suitable to describe the safe and sane strategy of that mature order of captains of industry who are governed by sound business principles. There is a certain bland sufficiency spread across the face of such a toad so circumstanced, while his comely personal bulk gives assurance of a pyramidal stability of principles (X, 109-10).

So the captain of industry came into the place of first consequence and took up the responsibilities of exemplar, philosopher and friend at large to civilized mankind; and no man shall say that he has not done as well as might be expected. Neither has he fallen short in respect of a becoming gravity through it all. The larger the proportion of the community's wealth and income which he has taken over, the larger the deference and imputation of merit imputed to him, and the larger and graver that affable condescension and stately benevolence that habitually adorn the character of the large captains of solvency. There is no branch or department of the humanities in which the substantial absentee owner is not competent to act as guide, philosopher and friend, whether in his own conceit or in the estimate of the underlying population,—in art and literature, in church and state, in science and education, in law and morals,—and the underlying population is well content. And nowhere does the pecuniary personage stand higher or more secure as the standard container of the civil virtues than in democratic America; as should be the case, of course, since America is the most democratic of them all. And nowhere else does the captain of big business rule the affairs of the nation, civil and political, and control the conditions of life so unreservedly as in democratic America; as should also be the case, inasmuch as the acquisition of absentee ownership is, after all, in the popular apprehension, the most meritorious and the most necessary work to be done in this country (X, 118).

There is nothing gained by finding fault with any of this businesslike enterprise that is bent on getting something for nothing, at any cost. After all, it is safe and sane business, sound and legitimate, and carried on blamelessly within the rules of the game. One may also dutifully believe that there is really no harm done, or at least that it might have been worse (VII, 84).

POLITICS AND GOVERNMENT

. . . any established order of law and custom is always out of date, in some degree. The code of right and honest living is always in arrears, by more or less; more so in the case of any people for whom the material conditions of life are in rapid process of change, as in America and the civilized countries of Europe (X, 18).

. . . all governmental establishments are necessarily conservative in all their dealings with [the] heritage of culture, except so far as they may be reactionary. Their office is the stabilization of archaic institutions, the measure of archaism varying from one to another (V, 331).

. . . [The] British arrangement for the control of national affairs by a body of interested gentlemen-investors has been, and perhaps still is, just as well at home in the affectionate preconceptions of the nineteenth-century British as the corresponding German usufruct by self-appointed swaggering aristocrats has been among the underlying German population, or as the American arrangement of national control by businessmen for business ends (V, 249).

The substantial interest of [the civil and military authorities] in the common welfare is of the same kind as the interest which a parasite has in the well-being of his host; a sufficiently substantial interest, no doubt, but there is in this relation nothing like a community of interest (V, 57).

. . . in the democratic commonwealth the common man has to be managed rather than driven,—except for minor groups of common men who live on the lower-common levels, and except for recurrent periods of legislative hysteria and judiciary blindstaggers. And it is pleasanter to be managed than to be driven. Chicane is a more humane art than corporal punishment (VII, 127).

A people whose workday ideal of self-help is unearned gain by legalized seizure at the cost of the community, who have been schooled in the practice of salesmanship until they believe that wealth is to be created by sharp practice, and that the perfect work of productive enterprise and initiative consists in "cornering the market" and "sitting tight,"—a body of men whose sense of the realities is palsied with this manner of hip-shotten logic is also fit to believe that "the foreigner pays the tax" imposed by a protective tariff or that a ship subsidy is of some benefit to someone else than the absentee owners of the ships. An illustrious politician has said that "you cannot fool all the people all the time," but in a case where the people in question are sedulously fooling themselves all the time the politicians can come near achieving that ideal result (X, 34).

. . . a degree of arrested spiritual and mental development is, in practical effect, no bar against entrance into public office. Indeed, a degree of puerile exuberance coupled with a certain truculent temper and boyish cunning is likely to command something of popular admiration and affection, which is likely to have a certain selective effect in the democratic choice of officials (XI, 435-36).

All is fair in war and politics. It is a game of force and fraud. There is said to be honor among thieves, but one does not look for such a thing among statesmen (X, 24).

PATRIOTISM AND NATIONALISM

The established order of law and custom which safe-guards absentee ownership in recent times and among civilized nations is, in the main, a modern creation; being, in effect, an outgrowth of usages and principles . . . which were induced by the conditions of life during early-modern times. The type-form of organized control by which this modern law and custom is upheld and enabled to function is that of the Nation—a politically self-determining body of people, legally and morally competent to make war.*

* There appears to be no other or further attribute or capacity that can be specified as a universally essential characteristic of the modern nation except this moral and legal license to resort to violence at will (X, 13).

Into this cultural and technological system of the modern world the patriotic spirit fits like dust in the eyes and sand in the bearings. Its net contribution to the outcome is obscuration, distrust, and retardation at every point where it touches the fortunes of modern mankind. Yet it is forever present in the counsels of the statesmen and in the affections of the common man, and it never ceases to command the regard of all men as the prime attribute of manhood and the final test of the desirable citizen (V, 40).

The patriotic spirit is at cross-purposes with modern life, but in any test case it is found that the claims of life yield before those of patriotism; and any voice that dissents from this order of things is as a voice crying in the wilderness (V, 41).

To give the fullest practical effect to the patriotic fervor that animates any modern nation, and so turn it to use in the most effective way, it is necessary to show that the demands of equity are involved in the case. . . . The common man must be persuaded that right is on his side. . . . The grounds of this conviction may often be tawdry enough, but the conviction is a necessary factor in the case. The requisite moral sanction may be had on various grounds, and, on the whole, it is not an extremely difficult matter to arrange (V, 36).

The higher the pitch of patriotic fervor, the more tenuous and more threadbare may be the requisite moral sanction. By cumulative excitation some very remarkable results have latterly been attained along this line (V, 38).

The only civilized nations that can be counted on as habitually peaceable are those who are so feeble or are so placed as to be cut off from hope of gain through contention. . . . If the peace is to be kept, therefore, it will have to be kept by and between peoples made up, in effect, of complete patriots; which comes near being a contradiction in terms. Patriotism is useful for breaking the peace, not for keeping it (V, 77-78).

There is, indeed, nothing to hinder a bad citizen being a good patriot; nor does it follow that a good citizen—in other respects—may not be a very indifferent patriot (V, 34).

CONSPICUOUS DISPLAY

. . . the utility of both [conspicuous leisure and conspicuous consumption] for the purposes of reputability lies in the element of waste that is common to both. In the one case it is a waste of time and effort, in the other it is a waste of goods (I, 85).

As increased industrial efficiency makes it possible to procure the means of livelihood with less labor, the energies of the industrious members of the community are bent to the compassing of a higher result in conspicuous expenditure, rather than slackened to a more comfortable pace. The strain is not lightened as industrial efficiency increases and makes a lighter strain possible, but the increment of output is turned to use to meet this want, which is indefinitely expansible . . . (I, 111).

It frequently happens that an element of the standard of living which sets out with being primarily wasteful, ends with becoming, in the apprehension of the consumer, a necessary of life; . . . [e.g.], carpets and tapestries, silver table service, waiter's services, silk hats, starched linen, many articles of jewelry and of dress (I, 99).

The skirt persists because it is cumbrous. It hampers the movements of the wearer and disables her, in great measure, for any useful occupation. So it serves as an advertisement (often disingenuous) that the wearer is backed by sufficient means to be able to afford the idleness, or impaired efficiency, which the skirt implies. The like is true of the high heel, and in less degree of several other features of modern dress (XI, 73).

. . . considered simply in their physical juxtaposition with the human form, the high gloss of a gentleman's hat or of a patent-leather shoe has no more of intrinsic beauty than a similarly high gloss on a threadbare sleeve; and yet . . . (I, 131-32).

It would be hazardous to assert that a useful purpose is ever absent from the utility of any article or of any service, however obviously its prime purpose and chief element is conspicuous waste; and it would be only less hazardous to assert of any primarily useful product that the element of waste is in no way concerned in its value, immediately and remotely (I, 101).

The cat is less reputable than [dogs and fast horses as a domestic animal]. . . , because she is less wasteful; she may even serve a useful end. At the same time the cat's temperament does not fit her for the honorific purpose. She lives with men on terms of equality, knows nothing of that relation of status which is the ancient basis of all distinctions of worth, honor, and repute, and she does not lend herself with facility to an invidious comparison between her owner and his neighbors. The exception to this last rule occurs in the case of such scarce and fanciful products as the Angora cat, which have some slight honorific value on the ground of expensiveness . . . (I, 140).

. . . the pervading principle and abiding test of good breeding is the requirement of a substantial and patent waste of time (I, 51).

MISCELLANY

It is the fortune even of good institutions to become imbecile with the change of conditioning circumstances, and it then becomes a question of their disestablishment, not of their rehabilitation. If there is anywhere a safe negative conclusion, it is that an institution grown mischievous by obsolescence need not be replaced by a substitute. . . . A man who loses a wart off the end of his nose does not apply to the *Ersatz* bureau for a convenient substitute (V, 215-16).

It would be extremely difficult to find a modern civilized residence or public building which can claim anything better than relative inoffensiveness in the eyes of anyone who will dissociate the elements of beauty from those of honorific waste. The endless variety of fronts presented by the better class of tenements and apartment houses in our cities is an endless variety of architectural distress and of suggestions of expensive discomfort. Considered as objects of beauty, the dead walls of the sides and back of these structures, left untouched by the hands of the artist, are commonly the best feature of the building (I, 154).

The first duty of a [newspaper] editor is to gauge the sentiments of his readers, and then tell them what they like to believe. By this he maintains or increases the circulation. His second duty is to see that nothing is said in the news items or editorials which may discountenance any claims or announcements made by his advertisers, discredit their standing or good faith, or expose any weakness or deception in any business venture that is or may become a valuable advertiser (II, 385-86).

Men like to believe that the personages whom they so admire by force of conventional routine are also of some use, as well as of great distinction,—that they even somehow contribute, or at least conduce, to the material well-being at large. Which is presumably to be set down as one of the wonders wrought by the instinct of workmanship, which will not let men be content without some colorable serviceability in the personages which they so create out of nothing-in-particular (X, 116-17).

It is also a matter of common notoriety and byword that in offences which result in a large accession of property to the offender he does not ordinarily incur the extreme penalty or the extreme obloquy with which his offence would be visited on the ground of the naïve moral code alone. The thief or swindler who has gained great wealth by his delinquency has a better chance than the small thief of escaping the rigorous penalty of the law; and some good repute accrues to him from his increased wealth and from his spending the irregularly acquired possessions in a seemly manner (I, 117).

. . . the traits that distinguish the swaggering delinquent and the punctilious gentleman of leisure from the common crowd are, in some measure, marks of an arrested spiritual development (I, 253).

BIBLIOGRAPHY

The listing that follows is made up entirely of books and it is divided into three sections: (A) books by Veblen, (B) books about Veblen, and (C) books written by those consciously and significantly influenced by Veblen. Only the first two of these categories are inclusive; the last is selective.

Because the text has utilized selections from all of Veblen's books, it was deemed unnecessary to provide annotation here; nor did it seem desirable or necessary to annotate the bibliography of the other two sections. Section (B) contains books that are both in praise and dispraise of Veblen; Section (C) contains books that have moved off from Veblen's own position in diverse ways.

In listing Veblen's own books, I have placed an asterisk after those still in print, and a double asterisk after those in print in inexpensive paperback editions. The Roman numerals designating Veblen's books correspond to the code used to identify quotations throughout this book. Where two publishers and publication dates are listed, they indicate the first and the most recent publication.

A. *Veblen's books.*

I. *The Theory of the Leisure Class.* New York: Macmillan, 1899. New York: New American Library, Mentor Edition, 1954. (**)

II. *The Theory of Business Enterprise.* New York: Scribner's, 1904. New York: New American Library, Mentor Edition, 1958. (**)

III. *The Instinct of Workmanship.* New York: B. W. Huebsch, 1914. New York: Viking, 1946.

IV. *Imperial Germany and the Industrial Revolution.* New York: Macmillan, 1915. New York: Viking, 1946.

V. *An Inquiry Into the Nature of Peace and the Terms of its Perpetuation.* New York: Macmillan, 1917. New York: Viking, 1945.

VI. *The Higher Learning in America, A Memorandum on the Conduct of Universities by Businessmen.* New York: B. W. Huebsch, 1918. New York: Sagamore Press, 1957. (**) (The Sagamore edition, which is paged differently than earlier printings, is the edition from which quotations in this book have been taken.)

VII. *The Vested Interests and the Common Man.* New York: B. W. Huebsch, 1919. New York: Viking, 1946. (When first issued, this book bore the title *The Vested Interests and the State of the Industrial Arts.*)

VIII. *The Place of Science in Modern Civilization.* New York: B. W. Huebsch, 1919. New York: Russell & Russell, 1961. (*)

IX. *The Engineers and the Price System.* New York: B. W. Huebsch, 1921. New York: Viking, 1947. (*)

X. *Absentee Ownership and Business Enterprise in Recent Times.* New York: B. W. Huebsch, 1923. New York: Viking, 1954.

XI. *Essays in Our Changing Order.* Edited by Leon Ardzrooni. New York: Viking, 1934. (*)

The two books that follow fall between the above category and that which follows. Both contain selections from Veblen's writings (articles and parts of books); both contain as well substantial introductory essays attempting to place and to evaluate Veblen.

Lerner, Max. *The Portable Veblen.* New York: Viking, 1948. (**)

Mitchell, Wesley Clair. *What Veblen Taught*. New York: Viking, 1945.

B. Books about Veblen.

The first work in this list is placed out of alphabetic order because it is a work of a different order of magnitude than those that follow. Dorfman's book is the definitive study of Veblen, which must be read by anyone seriously interested in the man or his works. It is a study that integrates Veblen with his times, and his ideas with both the man and the times. It also possesses a complete bibliography of Veblen's writings, from the most to the least important.

Dorfman, Joseph. *Thorstein Veblen and His America*. New York: Viking, 1934.

Daugert, Stanley Matthew. *The Philosophy of Thorstein Veblen*. New York: King's Crown Press, 1950.

Dobriansky, Lev E. *Veblenism, A New Critique*. Washington: Public Affairs Press, 1957.

Dowd, Douglas F. (ed.). *Thorstein Veblen: A Critical Reappraisal*. Ithaca: Cornell University Press, 1958.

Duffus, R. L. *The Innocents At Cedro, A Memoir of Thorstein Veblen and Some Others*. New York: Macmillan, 1944.

Hobson, John A. *Veblen*. New York: Wiley, 1937.

Riesman, David. *Thorstein Veblen, A Critical Interpretation*. New York: Scribner's, 1953.

Rosenberg, Bernard. *The Values of Veblen, A Critical Appraisal*. Washington: Public Affairs Press, 1956.

Schneider, Louis. *The Freudian Psychology and Veblen's Social Theory*. New York: King's Crown Press, 1948.

Teggart, Richard Victor. *Thorstein Veblen, A Chapter in American Economic Thought*. Berkeley: University of California Press, 1932.

C. *Books in the tradition of Veblen.*

Ayres, Clarence E. *The Theory of Economic Progress.* Chapel Hill: University of North Carolina Press, 1944.

Brady, Robert A. *Business as a System of Power.* New York: Columbia University Press, 1943.

——, *The Spirit and Structure of German Fascism.* New York: Viking, 1937.

——, *Organization, Automation, and Society, The Scientific Revolution in Industry.* Berkeley: University of California Press, 1961.

Clark, John M. *Studies in the Economics of Overhead Costs.* Chicago: University of Chicago Press, 1923.

——, *Social Control of Business.* Chicago: University of Chicago Press, 1926.

——, *Strategic Factors in Business Cycles.* New York: National Bureau of Economic Research, 1934.

Commons, John R. *Legal Foundations of Capitalism.* New York: Macmillan, 1924.

——, *Institutional Economics.* New York: Macmillan, 1934.

Copeland, Morris A. *A Study of Moneyflows in the United States.* New York: National Bureau of Economic Research, 1952.

——, *Fact and Theory in Economics.* In *Collected Papers,* edited by Chandler Morse. Ithaca: Cornell University Press, 1958.

Gambs, John S. *Beyond Supply and Demand, A Reappraisal of Institutional Economics.* New York: Columbia University Press, 1946.

Hamilton, Walton H. *The Pattern of Competition.* New York: Columbia University Press, 1940.

——, *et al. Price and Price Policies.* New York: McGraw-Hill, 1938.

Mills, C. Wright. *New Men of Power, America's Labor Leaders.* New York: Harcourt Brace, 1948.

——, *White Collar, The American Middle Classes.* New York: Oxford, 1951.

BIBLIOGRAPHY

——, *The Power Elite*. New York: Oxford, 1956.

Mitchell, Wesley Clair. *Business Cycles*. Berkeley: University of California Press, 1913.

Watkins, Myron W. *Industrial Combinations and Public Policy*. Boston: Houghton Mifflin, 1927.

——, with George W. Stocking. *Monopoly and Free Enterprise*. New York: Twentieth Century Fund, 1951.

INDEX

A

AEA *see* American Economic Association (AEA)

AFL *see* American Federation of Labor (AFL)

Absentee Ownership and Business Enterprise in Recent Times (Veblen), 13, 20, 30, 31, 41, 44

Ainu, 10-11

American Economic Association (AEA), 62n., 122n.

American Federation of Labor (AFL), 80

American Legion, 106

Andaman Islanders, 10-11

Argentina, 114

B

Bolshevism, 115

Brave New World (Huxley), 44

Brazil, 114

Business enterprise, 104
  advertising and, 108-9
  Bolshevism and, 115
  "captain of industry" in, 40
  change and, 32, 35-36
  competition in, 36
  corporations in, 41, 42-43
  corruption and, 50-51
  depression and, 110
  economics of, 40
  "free pecuniary contract" and, 34
  historical dilemma of, 52-53
  industrial democracy and, 108
  industrial development and, 37
  inside information and, 42
  machine process and, 51-52
  mergers and, 109
  morality of, 37
  natural rights and, 33-35
  peace and, 105
  politics and, 105
  Russian revolution and, 114-16

Business Week (Magazine), 62n.

C

Cameralism, 93n.

China, 113

Clark, John Bates, 63n.

Clark, John Maurice, 38n., 63n.

Colonialism, 112, 113

Commons, John R., 70

Communist Manifesto, The (Marx), 77

Coolidge, Calvin, 107

Critique of Political Economy, The (Marx), 57n.

D

Darwin, Charles, 23, 24, 57
Darwinism, 23-24
"Dementia Præcox" (Veblen), 101n., 106, 135
Dewey, John, 24

E

Economic Consequences of the Peace, 114
Economists, 129-30
  analytical frame work of, 145
  conventional, 143
  economic analysis and, 142-45
  neo-classical economics and, 142
  objectivity and, 144
  social problems and, 142
Education, 163
  architecture and, 170
  business principles in, 163-64
  captains of erudition and, 164-66
  college, 161
  deans, 166
  faculty, 168-70
  governing boards, 165
  professional school, 161-62, 163
  proposals, 172-73
  refuge, 170-72
  scholarship, 161
  student, 166-68
  teaching, 161
  university, 160-61, 162
Einstein, Albert, 57
Engineers and the Price Sys-
tem, The (Veblen), x, 153
England, 35, 88-89, 150, 184
Essays in Our Changing Order (Veblen), xiv, 22, 28, 29
European Common Market, 145, 148, 150

F

Fiscal policies, economic growth and, 143
France, 92n., 93n.

G

General Theory of Employment, Interest and Money (Keynes), 46
Germany, 80-81
  Communism in, 100n., 102
  industrialization of, 100, 116, 117
  Nazism in, 103
  patriotism in, 101, 102
  power struggle in, 102
  Social Democrats, 80-81, 100n., 102
  socialism in, 80-81
  Weimar Republic in, 101
  working class in, 100
Great Britain, 80, 103
  See also England
Guild Socialism, Veblen and, xvi

H

Harding, Warren, 107
Herdclitus, 57
Higher Learning in America,

The (Veblen), xiii, xiv, 72n.

Hofstadter, Richard, 23
  Social Darwinism in American Thought, 23n.

Hoover, Herbert, 107

I

IWW *see* Industrial Workers of the World (IWW)

Industry, 46
  capitalism and, 31, 45
  captain of, 40
  economics of, 40
  technology and, 32, 37, 38

Industrial capitalism, 31, 45

Industrial Workers of the World (IWW), 80

Industrialism, 39

Imperial Germany and the Industrial Revolution (Veblen), 22

Imperialism, 113

Innovations, social, 142

Inquiry into the Nature of Peace and the Terms of its Perpetuation, An (Veblen), xvi, 3, 11n.

Instinct of Workmanship, The (Veblen), 3, 26-28, 30, 58-59, 61-62

Institutions, formation of, 137

Investments, 47-48

Italy, fascism in, 103n.

J

James, William, 24

Japan, 99, 100
  fascism in, 103n.
  institutional deterioration in, 100

totalitarianism in, 102

Jevens, W. S., 63n.

Junkers, 94

K

Keynes, John Maynard, 47, 48, 69, 124
  Economic Consequences of the Peace, 114
  General Theory of Employment, Interest and Money, 46

Knight, Melvin M., xvii

Ku Klux Klan, 106

L

Labor, 48-49

Labour Party, 80

League of Nations, 104

Leisure class, 132-33
  as class of wealth, 14
  concepts of, 6
  conspicuous consumption and, 6-7, 9
  definition of, 7-8
  importance of appearance in, 14
  members of, 11-12
  non-leisure class and, 12
  origins of, 10
  pecuniary emulation and, 6-7, 9
  and politics, 17-18
  power and, 132-34
  property owners, 9
  as rulers, 10-11
  and social change, 18
  strata of, 15
  unproductiveness of, 8, 9

"vicarious leisure," 14
Loeb, Jacques, 24

M

Market system, economy and, 139
Marshall, Alfred, 63n., 67n.
Marx, Karl, 24, 25, 26, 32, 65, 121, 124, 131, 132
 class struggle theory, 48
 Communist Manifesto, The, 77
 Critique of Political Economy, The, 57n.
 relativistic viewpoint of, 57
 Veblen's critique of, 73-79, 80, 82-84
Marxian economics, 73, 82-84
 Germany and, 80-81
 metaphysical preconceptions and, 73-74
 private property and, 79
 rationality in, 75-76
 social change and, 74-75, 76
 technological change and, 77-78
 Veblen and, 24-25
Mason, E. S., 62n.
Menger, Carl, 63n.
Mergers, 40-41, 109
Mills, C. Wright, 133n.
 Power Elite, 133n.
Mitchell, Wesley Clair, 70
Modern Corporation and Private Property (Berle), 44
Monetary policies, economic growth and, 143

N

NLRA *see* National Labor Relations Act (NLRA)

Napoleonic Wars, 92
National Labor Relations Act (NLRA), 49
Nationalism, 147-48
"Natural Decay of Business Enterprise, The" (Veblen), 51
Neo-classical economics, 62, 72, 125
 analysis of, 127-28
 basic contributions of, 127
 choice of premises and, 129-30
 criticisms of, 126, 129-30
 development of, 70-71
 economic man and, 66
 "institutional variables" and, 128-29
 natural law and, 68
 optimal choice in, 125
 optimism of, 65
 problems contrasted to, 129
 production between 1929 and 1933 and, 69
 questions asked by, 63
 rational choice in, 129
 retrogression and, 130
 society and, 129, 130
 status quo and, 126-27
 supply and demand in, 67, 68
 welfare in, 125, 126, 127
New York Times (newspaper), 13n.
Newton, Isaac, 57
1984 (Orwell), 136

O

Opportunity of Japan, The (Veblen), 90n.
Organization Man (Whyte), 44

P

Panem et circenses: The Bread Line and the Movies (Veblen), 111
"Passing of National Frontiers, The" (Veblen), 104n.
Patriotism, 147-48
Peace, 97-98
  United States and, 103-4
"Peace and the Price System" (Veblen), 149
Place of Science in Modern Civilization, The (Veblen), xivn., 5-6, 20, 26, 56, 58, 62, 64-66, 73-82
Prussia, 92
Politics, international, 135-36
Power Elite (Mills), 133n.

R

Radicalism, 1
Riesman, David, 124
"Robinson Crusoe economics" *see* Neo-classical economics

S

Smith, Adam, 33, 65, 70
Social Darwinism in American Thought (Hofstadter), 23n.
Social Democrats, 80-81
Social evolution, 19
"Social" problems, modern, 138-39
Specialization, 136
Spencer, Herbert, 23
State, theory of, 134
  modern technology and, 135-36

vested interests and, 134
Sumner, William Graham, 23

T

"Technocrats," 55
Technology, industrial, 32, 37, 38
Theory of Business Enterprise, The (Veblen), 3, 20, 31, 32-41, 42-44, 46-53, 56
Theory of the Leisure Class, The (Veblen), 3, 6-19, 21-23, 78
Thermonuclear war, prevention of, 135-36
Thirty Years' War, 91-92
Todas, 10-11
Treaty of Versailles, 114

U

Union of Soviet Socialist Republics (USSR), 114-17, 128n.
United States of America, 104, 105-7
  international politics and, 112
  patriotism and, 107
  peace and, 103-5
  Secret Service of, 106
  technology and, 156

V

Veblen, Thomas, 4
Veblen, Thorstein
  Absentee Ownership and Business Enterprise in Recent Times, 13, 20, 30, 31, 41, 44

Veblen, Thorstein (*cont.*)
advertising and, 108-109
aims of, 2
anthropological theories of, 6
approach of, 125
birth of, 1, 4
business enterprise and, 104, 139-41
Bolshevism and, 115
"captain of industry" in, 40
change and, 32, 35-36
competition in, 36
corporations in, 41, 42-43
corruption and, 50-51
depression and, 110
economics of, 40
"free pecuniary contract" and, 34
historical dilemma of, 52-53
industrial democracy and, 108
industrial development and, 37
inside information and, 42
machine process and, 51-52
mergers and, 109
morality of, 37
natural rights and, 33-35
peace and, 105
politics and, 105
Russian revolution and, 114-16
characteristics of, 121-22, 123, 124, 130
childhood of, 1-2
on conflict, 19
conspicuous consumption, 6-7, 9, 13, 155-56

critique style of, 120
on Darwinism, 23-24
"Dementia Præcox," 101n., 106, 135
democratic society and, 120, 121
depression and, 44, 45-49
on destructive elements, 20-21
economic history and, 156-57
economic scope and, 5-6
education of, 4-5
architecture and, 170
business principles in, 163-64
captains of erudition, 164-66
college, 161
deans, 166
faculty, 168-70
governing boards, 165
professional school, 161-62, 163
proposals, 172-73
refuge, 170-72
scholarship, 161
student, 166-68
teaching, 161
university, 160-61, 162
Engineers and the Price System, The, xiv, 153
on England, 88-89, 184
Essays in Our Changing Order, xiv, 22, 28, 29
evolutionary views of, 29
family background, 3
free trade and, 145
Germany, 86
bureaucracy and, 93
cameralism and, 93n.
Communism in, 100n., 102
economic development of, 89, 95

historical conditioning in, 90

industrialization of, 88, 89, 93-95

industrialization of, 100, 116-117

Junkers and, 91, 94

military and, 95

Napoleonic Wars and, 92

natural resources and, 94-95

Nazism in, 103

patriotism in, 101, 102

power struggle in, 102

Prussia and, 91, 92

race and, 90

Social Democrats, 100n., 102

Thirty Years' War and, 91-92

transportation and, 89-90, 96

Weimar Republic in, 101

working class in, 100

World War I and, 96-97

Zollverein and, 89

Guild Socialism and, xvi

Higher Learning in America, The, xiii, xiv, 72n.

"honorific calculation" and, 9

on idle curiosity, 20

Imperial Germany and the Industrial Revolution, 22

industrial capitalism, 31, 45

industrial democracy and, 108

"industrial democracy" and, 120, 121

industry and, 140, 141

influences on, 22-24

Inquiry Into the Nature of Peace and the Terms of its

Perpetuation, An, xvi, 3, 11n.

on instinct, 26-28

Instinct of Workmanship, The, 3, 26-28, 30, 58-59, 61-62

institutions and, 121, 144, 145

Japan

fascism in, 103n.

institutional deterioration in, 100

totalitarianism in, 102

learning process and, 120

leisure class

as class of wealth, 14

concepts of, 6

conspicuous consumption and, 6-7, 9

definition of, 7-8

importance of appearance in, 14

members of, 11-12

and non-leisure class, 12

origins of, 10

pecuniary emulation and, 6-7, 9

and politics, 17-18

property owners, 9

as rulers, 10-11

and social change, 18

strata of, 15

unproductiveness of, 8, 9

"vicarious leisure," 14

on major institutions, 20

Marx compared to, 24-25

Marxian economics, 73, 82-84

Germany and, 80-81

metaphysical preconceptions and, 73-74

private property and, 79

rationality in, 75-76

Veblen, Thorstein (*cont.*)
  social change and, 74-75, 76
  technological change and, 77-78
  modern technology and, 38-39, 135-36
  nation state and, 147
  nationalism and, 104, 147-48
  neo-classical economics, 62, 72, 125
    analysis of, 127-28
    basic contributions of, 127
  neo-classical economics
    choice of premises and, 129-30
    criticisms of, 126, 129-30
    development of, 70-71
    economic man and, 66
    "institutional variable" and, 128-29
    natural law and, 68
    optimal choice in, 125
    optimism of, 65
    problems contrasted to, 129
    production between 1929 and 1933 and, 69
    questions asked by, 63
    rational choice in, 129
    rationality in, 64-65
    retrogression and, 130
    society and, 129, 130
    status quo and, 126-27
    supply and demand in, 67, 68
    welfare in, 125, 126, 127
  objectivity of, xii-xiii, 3
  obscurity of, xi
  Opportunity of Japan, The, 90n.
  "pacific league of nations," 97, 103-4

"*Panem et circenses:* The Bread Line and the Movies," 111
"Passing of National Frontiers, The," 104n.
patriotism and, 98, 101, 147-48
peace, 97-98
  United States and, 103-4
"Peace and the Price System," 149
pecuniary emulation, 6-7, 9, 13
personal life of, 123
pessimism and, 29-30, 121-22, 124, 130
Place of Science in Modern Civilization, The, xivn., 5-6, 20, 26, 56, 58, 62, 64-66, 73-82
politics, 105
principles of action and, 144
protective tariffs and, 145-46
psychological theories of, 6
purpose of, 121, 156-58
radicalism and, 1
"ruling class" and, 132, 133
self respect and, 7, 13
serviceability, 37-38
social change and, 4, 121, 145
as social critic, 131
on social evolution, 19
social science and, xi, 119-20
on status quo, 21
structural change and, 144
tariffs and, 105
as teacher, 122
theoretical criticism of, 131-32
Theory of Business Enterprise, The, 3, 20, 31, 32-

41, 42-44, 46-53, 56, 108, 109
Theory of the Leisure Class, The, 3, 6-19, 21-23, 78
theory of state, 134-36
three-fold interest of, 152
unlearning and, 120
values of, 22
Veblenisms
  on admiration, 189
  armaments and war, 175-78
  on buildings, 189
  business versus industry, 178-83
  conspicuous display, 187-88
  on duty of newspaper editors, 189
  dynastic state, 175
  on institutions, 188-89
  patriotism and nationalism, 185-87
  politics and government, 183-85
  property accession, 189-90
  salesmanship, 173-74
  on spiritual development, 190

sports, 174
vested interests and, 21
Vested Interests and the Common Man, The, xiv, 61, 67-68
virtues of American economy and, 140
weaknesses of, 124
wit of, xii
working class and, 17
on workmanship, 20
writings of, xii-xiv
writings of, 122, 123-24

W

Walgas, Léon, 63n.
"Welfare economics" *see* Neoclassical economics
Wilson, Woodrow, 104
World peace, prospects for, 135-36
World War I, 92, 95, 96-97

Z

Zollverein, 89